T0329011

BIBLIOGRAPHY

OF

ENGLISH LANGUAGE
AND LITERATURE
1920

.·.

COMPILED BY MEMBERS OF
THE MODERN HUMANITIES
RESEARCH ASSOCIATION

.·.

Now published
AT THE UNIVERSITY PRESS
CAMBRIDGE

LONDON
CAMBRIDGE UNIVERSITY PRESS
FETTER LANE
E.C. 4

CAMBRIDGE
UNIVERSITY PRESS

University Printing House, Cambridge CB2 8BS, United Kingdom

Cambridge University Press is part of the University of Cambridge.

It furthers the University's mission by disseminating knowledge in the pursuit of education, learning and research at the highest international levels of excellence.

www.cambridge.org
Information on this title: www.cambridge.org/9781316601792

© Cambridge University Press 1921

First published 1921
First paperback edition 2015

A catalogue record for this publication is available from the British Library

ISBN 978-1-316-60179-2 Paperback

PREFACE

THIS BIBLIOGRAPHY represents the beginning of a task which the Modern Humanities Research Association hopes in time to accomplish—that of providing modern language scholars and students with adequate and up-to-date bibliographies year by year. For the first year it was thought best to limit the field, and the present pamphlet therefore represents only work published on English language and literature during the year 1920. The countries represented in it are as follows: Australia, British Isles, Canada, Czecho-Slovakia, Denmark, France, Germany, Holland, India, Italy, Portugal, Rumania, Serbia, Spain (including works in Catalan), Sweden, Switzerland, and the United States of America. Both books and articles are included in the list; the aim has been to include all serious contributions to the subject, and the task of selection has generally been left to the local compiler. From time to time however expert opinion has been called in as to the merits of any book or article. All works not published during the year 1920 are excluded, and a supplement will be published in the Association's Bulletin for July 1921, containing any titles which arrived too late for inclusion.

The organisation of such work as this is not easy, and it so happens that the unusual pressure of University work upon the principal compilers has made it impossible to prepare this pamphlet with the care which it is hoped to give to its successors. We print on p. vi the instructions to collaborators to the Bibliography for 1921, and we hope that our critics will not only send in suggestions, but will become compilers as well. The incompleteness of the present issue is due entirely to a dearth of helpers: it is our eventual aim to build up a strong body of reliable compilers in every country for each of the languages studied there.

PREFACE

The names of the compilers for 1920 are as follow in alphabetical order: Mr A. F. G. Bell, M. Beza, Prof. G. Bonnard, Prof. S. J. Crawford, Sr. Estelrich, Mr J. A. Falconer, Dr B. Fehr, Prof. A. S. Ferguson, Dr F. de Figueiredo, Mr B. J. Hayes, Prof. A. Koszul, Mr P. R. Krishnawami, Miss Ràdmila Lotić, Prof. V. Mathesius, Prof. C. S. Northup, Miss A. C. Paues, Mr E. Allison Peers, Prof. P. Popovič, Mr J. Purves, Prof. L. Schücking, Sr. Solalinde, Miss Zora Vulović, Dr R. E. Zachrisson, Mr R. W. Zandvoort. In addition to these are seven helpers who wish to remain anonymous, including one who kindly undertook to collect the British contributions, and, in addition, in spite of unusual pressure, gave much help with the arrangement of the slips. Should any name have been omitted by inadvertence from the list it will be published in the next issue.

E. ALLISON PEERS.

MODERN HUMANITIES RESEARCH ASSOCIATION

President 1920–1.

PROFESSOR OTTO JESPERSEN, PH.D., LITT.D.

Past Presidents.

1918–19. SIR SIDNEY LEE, LITT.D.   1919–20. M. GUSTAVE LANSON.

Chairman of Committee.

PROFESSOR F. S. BOAS, M.A., LL.D.

<table>
<tr><td>Sub-Secretary for France.</td><td>Sub-Secretary for America.</td></tr>
<tr><td>MISS M. D. MACKIE,
84 Rue d'Assas, Paris.</td><td>G. L. VAN ROOSBROECK, Esq.
University of Minnesota,
Minneapolis, U.S.A.</td></tr>
<tr><td>Hon. Treasurer.</td><td>Hon. Secretary.</td></tr>
<tr><td>B. W. DOWNS, Esq.,
Christ's College, Cambridge.</td><td>E. ALLISON PEERS, Esq.,
The University, Liverpool.</td></tr>
</table>

IT may not be out of place to give in brief form the aims of our Association and the way in which those who use this bibliography may join it.

The Association was founded on June 1st, 1918, and at present numbers over 600 members. Its main object is the encouragement of advanced study in Modern Languages and Literatures by co-operation, through correspondence, personal intercourse, the interchange of information and counsel, and financial support for students engaged in research. The Association aims at improving and facilitating means and methods, and seeks such a co-ordination of isolated effort that those interested or engaged in the same branch of research shall be kept informed of each other's work, and that unnecessary duplication of energy shall be avoided.

Membership of the Association is open to graduate students of all countries, at the discretion of the Committee. Approved

Institutions and Associations may become members as well as individuals. A quarterly Bulletin is published, describing the proceedings and activities of the Association; members may also join the Modern Language Association of America and purchase the *Modern Language Review* at a reduced subscription. Groups of members with similar interests may be formed within the Association.

The M.H.R.A. further: (i) puts members who have interest in cognate subjects into touch with one another through the Secretary; (ii) collects and circulates information and suggestions likely to be of permanent use to research students; (iii) procures specialised information for members who are prevented from making personal investigations; (iv) organises co-operative research on the part of those who have not the opportunities to do much individual work. It hopes, as soon as funds permit, (v) to undertake publication of original work, (vi) to found bursaries and scholarships for the furtherance of its objects.

Persons duly qualified for membership of the Association may become:

1. Ordinary members, if actually engaged in or contemplating research.

2. Associate members, if in sympathy with the aims of the Association, but not personally engaged in research.

The minimum annual subscription for ordinary and associate members is 7s. 6d. (12 francs; $2), payable to the Hon. Treasurer on or before the 1st of October in each year for the academic year ending on the following 30th of September. The Association is federated to the Modern Language Associations of England and America; members of these Associations pay 6s. and $1.50 respectively as their annual subscription to the M.H.R.A.

Applications for membership should be addressed to the Hon. Secretary: E. Allison Peers, M.A., The University, Liverpool.

INSTRUCTIONS FOR COLLABORATORS

1. The first list of books and articles, as complete as possible, is asked for by Nov. 1, 1921. This will enable us to get forward with the bulk of the classification and ensure the early appearance of the work.

2. The second list must be in by Jan. 31, 1922. Notices received after this date cannot be inserted in the 1922 volume, though they will be published in the *Bulletin*, if space allows, as a supplementary list.

3. The following details should if known be given. Concerning books: Author, full title, no. of pages, size of page (in centimetres), publisher, price. Concerning articles: Author, full title, journal (name, volume, number, date), nos. of pages.

4. It will be very helpful if cards or slips of paper (5″ × 3″, *i.e.* 12·5 cm. × 7·5 cm.) are used. One notice only should be written on each.

5. Arrange data thus:
   Jones, Henry Charles.
       History of English Literature.
ix + 623 pp., 19 × 12·5, Allen and Brown. Edinburgh. 6s. 6d. Reviewed by R. C. Smith, Engl. Stud. 54. 3–5.

6. The divisions of subject in this year's bibliography should be followed except as special notice is given.

7. The aim of the Bibliography is to include all serious contributions to the subject. Brief mentions will generally be excluded, and articles which make no pretence at being of a scholarly nature. Where there is doubt collaborators are asked to write the notice, adding a short description of its scope by which the Editors may estimate its worth.

8. Any other concise annotations will be of value: though space may not permit of their publication, they will be available for reference by members wishing to consult them.

9. Work dealing with the influence of English on other languages and literatures or *vice versâ* should be included.

10. The title of any journal which cannot be consulted but is thought worthy of examination should be sent in as soon as possible.

All notices and communications should be addressed to
E. ALLISON PEERS,
THE UNIVERSITY,
LIVERPOOL.

CONTENTS

A. GENERAL

B. ENGLISH LANGUAGE

C. ENGLISH LITERATURE

A. GENERAL

I. BIBLIOGRAPHY

1. Athena: A Year Book of the Learned World. The English Speaking Races. Edited by C. A. Ealand. 8vo. pp. 400. Black. 15s.

2. CROSS, T. P. A List of Books and Articles, Chiefly Bibliographical, Designed to Serve as an Introduction to the Bibliography and Methods of English Literary History. Chicago. University of Chicago Bookstore. (With an Index.) 1920. 19·6 × 13·4 cm. pp. viii + 53. Interleaved.

3. GREENLAW, E. and MOFFATT, J. S. Recent Literature [on the Elizabethan Period]. Studies in Philology, April 1920, XVII, 246–68.

4. Jahresbericht über die Erscheinungen auf dem Gebiete der Germanischen Philologie (ed. by Gesellschaft für Deutsche Philologie in Berlin). Vols. 39 and 40 in one, 1917, 1918. Leipzig, Reisland, 1920. M. 30. (English, II, 29–56.)

5. The Literary Who's Who (formerly 'Literary Year Book') for the year 1920. $8\frac{3}{11}$ × $5\frac{3}{4}$. pp. xxxii + 376. Routledge. 8s. 6d.

6. The New Calendar of Great Men. Edited by Frederic Harrison, S. H. Swinny and F. S. Marvin. New Ed. Revised and Enlarged. 8vo. pp. 730. Macmillan. 30s.

7. Poetry Society of America: Books by Twentieth Century Poets. In the Library Journal, Feb. 1, 1920. XLV. 110.

8. A Reference Library: English Language and Literature (English Association Pamphlet, No. 46). 8vo. Oxford Univ. Press. 1s.

9. ROBERTS, R. A. The Reports of the Historical MSS. Commission. 'Helps for Students of History,' No. 22. Cr. 8vo. pp. 91. S.P.C.K. 2s. 6d.

II. BIOGRAPHY

1. BOYS, A. M. Contemporary Poets: a Classified List. In Bulletin of Bibliography, November 1919, August 1920, X, 136–9, XI, 10–12, 28–9. Also reprinted by the F. W. Foxon Co., Boston. pp. 8.

2. Chambers' Biographical Dictionary. The Great of all Times and Nations. Ed. by David Patrick and Francis Hindes Groom. 8vo. pp. 1010. Chambers. 15s.

3. LEE, Sir S. The Dictionary of National Biography, 1901–1911. The Second Supplement. 8vo. pp. 2082. Milford. 36s.

4. MUSS-ARNOLT, W. The Scottish Service Book of 1637 and its Successors: a Bio-Bibliographical Study. Amer. Journal of Theology, July 1920, XXIV, 386–406.

5. THAYER, W. R. The Art of Biography. New York. Scribners. 1920. 19·5 cm. pp. x + 155. Reviewed in The Weekly Review, Nov. 3, 1920, III, 425–6.

B. ENGLISH LANGUAGE

III. VOCABULARY

III. (a) DICTIONARIES

1. A New English Dictionary. Edited by Sir James Murray, Henry Bradley, W. A. Craigie and C. T. Onions. Vol. x, Ti–Z. New Section, Visor–Vywer, by W. A. Craigie. Milford. 2s. 6d.

2. ANSTED, A. A Dictionary of Sea Terms. 7½ × 5. pp. 324. J. Brown. 7s. 6d.

3. Blackie's Compact Etymological Dictionary. Prepared by R. J. Cunliffe. 8vo. pp. 380. Blackie. 2s.

4. BONNAFFÉ, E. Dictionnaire étymologique et historique des anglicismes. 13 × 21. pp. 200. Delagrave, Paris. 13 f.

III. (b) WORD STUDY

5. BASKETT, W. D. Parts of the Body in the later Germanic Dialects. pp. ix + 139. Chicago Univ. Press.

6. BLAU, E. 'Payndemayn': zu Chaucer's Tale of Sir Topas. See VIII, 22.

7. CRABB, G. Crabb's English Synonyms. Centenary edition. With an introduction by John H. Finlay. 8 × 5¾. pp. x + 717. Routledge. 6s.

8. DEY, W. M. A Note on Old French Por in English. Stud. in Phil. Univ. N. Carolina, XVIII, 1, Jan.

9. EKWALL, E. Zu zwei keltischen Lehnwörtern im Altenglischen (funta, torr). Engl. Stud. 54, 102–111.

10. EMERSON, O. F. Mead—Meadow, Shade—Shadow, a Study in Analogy. Modern Language Notes, XXXV, 3, 147–154, March 1920.

10a. —— M. E. Clannesse. P. M. Lang. Ass. Am. XXIV, 3.

11. EYKMAN, L. P. H. Round—Around. De Drie Talen, Jan. 1920.

12. FOWLER, H. W. Moral(e). Times Lit. Suppl., Feb. 19, 1920.

13. GOODE, J. Hawk—Heronshaw (Hamlet ii, 2). Times Lit. Suppl., Feb. 26, 1920.

14. HOLTHAUSEN, F. Etymologisches (u.a. Westfäl. küllen, ne. kill, mnd. dobbe, ne. dub). P. Br. B. 44, 473–483.

14a. —— Wortdeutungen. Engl. Stud. 54, 87–92.

15. HORN, W. Zur altenglischen Wortgeschichte (milc, geare). Archiv für d. Stud. d. N. Spr. 140, 107.

16. JESPERSEN, O. Dansk håbe, eng. hope, tysk hoffen. Nord. Tidskr. f. fil. VIII, 151–2 (1920).

17. KIRKERS, E. Altenglisch þám, þæm 'dem, den' (Dat. Pl.). Ae. héo 'sie' (Nom. Sing. F.) und híe 'sie' (Nom. Plur.)—Ae. þir 'dieses.' —Westsächs. iernan 'laufen' und biernan 'brennen.' Idg. Forschgen, 38, 213–217.

18. KROESCH, S. Semantic Notes. Journal of English and Germanic Philol., Jan. 1920, XIX, 86–93.

19. LANGENFELT, G. *Danzig* och *Dansk*. Ett geografiskt och filologiskt misstag. Finsk Tidskrift, 88, 63–79 (1920).

19a. —— 2. En fornengelsk tvebottnetjärn ('twybytme del' Birch, Cart. Sax. 3, pp. 116 f.). 3. Fornengelskt *Vrindesholt* (Cod. Dipl. Ævi Sax. ed. Kemble, III, 320). 4. *Assedun*, ett tillägg. In 'Namn och Bygd,' VIII, 82 f. Article 'Växjö och andra Ortnamn.'

19b. —— Toponymics or Derivations from Local Names in English. 23 × 15 pp. 252. Appelbergs Boktryckeri A.–B. Upsala. 15 kr.

20. LIEBERMANN, F. *Shute* mittelenglisch: *Lastschiff*. Archiv, 140, 263. Der Ausdruck *Leet* (to Anglia, Beibl. 31, 85 note). Anglia, Beibl. 31, 237–8.

21. LILJEGREN, S. B. Two American Words (*pod, perky*). Anglia, Beibl. 31, 67–9.

22. LOANE, G. G. A Thousand and One Notes on 'A New English Dictionary.' 8¼ × 5¼. pp. 64. 4 Linnel Close, N.W. 4. 5s.

23. MONTGOMERY, M. *Cursed Hebenon* (or *Hebona*) (to Hamlet, I, v, 62). Mod. Lang. Rev. 15, 304–306.

24. POLLARD, A. F. The Word *State*. Times Lit. Suppl., Sept. 23, 1920. Cf. Evolution of Meaning, *ib.* E. Barker; *ib.* Sept. 16. H. C. Dowdall.

25. POUTSMA, H. *To meet* and *to meet with* compared. De Drie Talen, Jan. 1920.

26. RITTER, O. Beiträge zur englischen Wortkunde (ae. *botl*, schott. *cook*, ne. *crimine, criminy*, ae. *cume*(*n*)*dre*, *ȝende, ofost, trūs,* *ȝȳl(e)*). Engl. Stud. 54, 92–102.

27. RÖSLER, M. Veraltete Wörter in der 'Grammatica Anglicana' von 1594. Engl. Stud. 53, 2, Dec.

28. RUUD, M. B. A Conjecture Concerning the Origin of Modern English *She*. Modern Language Notes, XXXV, 222–225, April 1920.

29. SAMPSON, J. An Arme-Gaunt Steede (to Ant. and Cleop. I, v). Times Lit. Suppl., April 29, 1920.

30. SCHLUTTER, O. B. Is there sufficient evidence to warrant the authenticity of O.E. *treppan*, 'to trap'? Neophilologus, V, 351. pp. 4.

31. —— Weitere Beiträge zur altenglischen Wortforschung. Anglia, 44, 94–96 and 291–296.

32. SCHWENTNER, E. Ags. *óleccan* 'schmeicheln.' P. Br. B. 44, 500–501.

33. SMITH, C. A. New Words Self-Defined. New York, Doubleday, Page & Co. 1919. 19·5 cm. pp. viii + 215, [1]. Rev. in The Nation, March 6, 1920, CX, 305–6.

34. SUNDÉN, K. F. Några förbisedda skandinaviska lånord i Sir Gawayne and the Grene Knyȝt. Minnesskrift utg. av Filogiska Samfundet, Gothenburg.

35. SWAEN, A. E. H. Contributions to Old English Lexicography X, XI. Engl. St. 53, 353–362 and 54, 337–52.

36. WALLENBERG, J. Me. *fled(de)*, ne. *fled* [pret. tense of 'to flee']. Anglia, Beibl. 31, 221–3.

4 BIBLIOGRAPHY

III. (c) NAME STUDY

37. ALLEN, E. L. The Devil's Property in the United States. The Outlook, Oct. 6, 1920, CXXVI, 246–7. On place-names.

38. BJÖRKMAN, E. Skialf och Skilfing, Namn och Bygd, VII, 164–81. (Deals also with the *Scylfingas* of Beowulf.)

39. —— Hæþcyn und Hákon. Engl. Stud. 54, 24–35.

40. —— Studien über die Eigennamen im Beowulf. *See* Beowulf. VII, 19.

41. EKWALL, G. Scandinavians and Celts in the North-west of England. In Festskrift of the Univ. of Lund, 1918. Rev. by O. B. Schlutter in Jour. of Eng. and Germ. Philol., July 1920, XIX, 422–3.

42. HARRISON, H. Surnames of the United Kingdom. A Concise Etymological Dictionary. London: Moorland Press. 2 vols. 50s.

43. HINZE, O. Studien zu Ben Jonson's Namengebung in seinen Dramen. Leipziger Diss. 1918, pp. 84. 8°.

44. LAWRENCE, F. W. The Origin of American State Names. In The National Geographic Mag., Aug. 1920, XXXVIII, 105–43. Illus.

45. MAWER, A. The Place-Names of Northumberland and Durham. (Cambridge Archæological and Ethnological Series.) Cambridge Univ. Press. 8vo. pp. x + 271. (1920). 20s. Reviewed Times Lit. Suppl., Feb. 10, 1921, cf. Letters, *ib.* Feb. 17th and 24th.

46. RITTER, O. Über einige Ortsnamen aus Lancashire. Engl. Stud. 54, 187–194.

47. SCHÜCKING, L. L. Wiðergyld (Beowulf 2051). *See* Beowulf.

48. UPHAM, W. Minnesota Geographic Names: Their Origin and Historic Significance. St Paul, Minn. The Minnesota Historical Soc. 1920. 23 cm. pp. [iv], viii + 735. Rev. by M. R. Gilmore in Minn. History Bulletin, Aug. 1920, III, 448–9.

49. WOOD, F. A. Names of Stinging, Gnawing, and Rending Animals. i. Amer. Jour. Philol. XLI, 223–39, 336–54.

IV. HISTORY OF LANGUAGE AND GRAMMAR

IV. (a) GENERAL

1. BRADLEY, H. On the Relations between Spoken and Written Language, with special reference to English. Cr. 8vo. 36 pp. 2s. Oxford Univ. Press. Rev. Times Lit. Suppl., Jan. 8, 1920.

2. BRAHDE, A. Studier over engelske Præpositioner, En principiel Undersögelse. Copenhagen, Schönberg. 5 kr.

3. CHAPLIN, A. The Romance of Language. 8vo. 8 × 5¼. pp. 245. London, Sidgwick and Jackson. 7s. 6d.

4. COLTON, A. Gains and Losses in Language. Harper's Mag., Apr. 1920, CXL, 707–9.

5. DRIGGS, H. R. Our Living Language: How to Teach It and How to Use It. Lincoln, Nev., The University Publishing Company. 1920. 19·7 × 13 cm. pp. x + 302.

6. FRANZ, W. Grammatisches in Shakespeare. Engl. Stud. 54, 1, March. Cf. IV, 55.

7. GRANDGENT, C. H. Old and New, Sundry Papers. Cambridge, Harvard Univ. Press. 1920. 21·1 × 14·6 cm. pp. 177. Contents: Nor Yet the New. Fashion and the Broad A. The Dog's Letter. Numeric Reform in Nescioubia. Is Modern Language Teaching a Failure? The Dark Ages. New England Pronunciation. School. Reviewed by T. P. Cross in Modern Philology, Aug. 1920, XVIII, 231–2; in The Weekly Review, Oct. 13, 1920.

8. HÜBNER, W. John Locke als Sprachphilosoph. Die Neueren Sprachen, 27, 385–6.

9. HUGHES, R. Our Statish Language. In Harper's Mag., May 1920, CXL, 846–9.

10. KELLOGG, W. G. Is Grammar Useless? In The No. Amer. Rev., July 1920, CCXII, 36–42.

11. MASTER, F. D. English Words Discriminated, being a collection of important Synonyms, Paronyms, Doublets, etc., with explanation, etc. pp. 132. N. M. Tripáthi, for N. M. Tripáthi & Co., Bombay (June 1920). Royal 12mo, 2nd Ed. Re. 1.

12. MATTHEWS, B. American English and British English. In Scribner's Mag., Nov. 1920. LXVIII, 621–6.

12 a. —— The Latest Novelties in Language. In Harper's Mag., June 1920, CXLI, 82–7.

12 b. —— The Mongrelian Language. In Scribner's Mag., Aug. 1920, LXVIII, 219–21.

13. MURSELL, J. L. Analysis of the Concept of Meaning. In The Philosophical Rev., May 1920, XXIX, 256–68.

14. NICKLIN, T. The Sounds of Standard English. Oxford Univ. Press. 3s.

15. O'NEILL. A Guide to the English Language. Its history, development and use. London: Jack. viii + 455 pp.

16. Report on the Terminology and Classifications of Grammar. Oriental Advisory Committee. 8vo. Oxford Univ. Press. 3s. 6d.

17. SARGEAUNT, J. The Pronunciation of English Words derived from the Latin. S.P.G. Tract No. IV. Oxford Univ. Press. 2s. 6d.

18. TRUEBLOOD, T. C. The Spoken English of Australasia. In Quart. Jour. Speech Education, Apr. 1920, VI, 2, 1–10.

19. UTTER, R. P. The Case Against Grammar. In Harper's Mag., Feb. 1920, CXL, 407–13.

20. WALLIS, G. The Philosophy of Speech. London: Allen and Unwin. 7s. 6d.

21. WILLIAMS, F. Newspaper English. In The No. Amer. Rev., Nov. 1920, CCXII, 631–40.

22. WILLIS, G. The Philosophy of Speech. Cr. 8vo. 7$\frac{3}{11}$ × 5$\frac{1}{4}$. pp. 256. G. Allen and Unwin. 7s. 6d.

23. ZACHRISSON, R. E. The World Language. English most suitable. An Inquiry by The Northern Peace Union. Svenska freds- och skiljedoms-föreningens förlag, Stockholm. Kr. 2.

24. ZACHRISSON, R. E. Grammatical Changes in Present-Day English. Studier i Modern Språkvetenskap utg. av Nyfilologiska Sänskapet, Stockholm, VII, 1920. pp. 43.

25. —— Engelska Stilarter. Stockholm: A. V. Carlson. 1920. 175 pp. 4·50 kr.

IV. (b) GENERAL AND HISTORICAL GRAMMARS

26. ALVAREZ ARANDA and RAMSPATT, Y. C. Curso de lengua inglesa. 2° curso. Madrid. 4°. 132 pp. 6 ptas.

27. FAULDING, G. M. A Constructive Grammar of Present Day English: being a 3 years' course of study of the English Language for Indian students. pp. x + 156. K. and J. M. Cooper, Bombay, 1920. Crown 8vo. Price, Rs. 1.

28. LUICK, K. Historische Grammatik der englischen Sprache. 3. u. 4. Lieferung (bis S. 448). Leipzig. 6 Mk u. 8 Mk.

29. MOORE, S. and THOMAS, A. K. The Elements of Old English. Ann Arbor, Mich.: Geo. Wahr. 1919. 19·9 × 14 cm. pp. vii + 209. Reviewed by J. R. Hulbert in Modern Philology, May 1920, XVIII, 63–4.

30. MOORE, S. Historical Outlines of English Phonology and Middle English Grammar, for Courses in Chaucer, Middle English, and the History of the English Language. Ann Arbor, Mich.: Geo. Wahr. 1919. 25·5 × 17 cm. pp. viii + 83. Reviewed by J. R. H[ulbert] in Modern Philology, May 1920, XVIII, 63–4.

31. Ross, R. W. Practical English Grammar. Book I. pp. viii + 68. K. and J. M. Cooper, Bombay. Crown 8vo. 2nd Ed. Price, Rs. 7.

32. STURTEVANT, E. H. An Introduction to the Historical Study of Language. Univ. Chicago Press. $ 1.

33. THOMAS, P. G. An Introduction to the History of the English Language. 8vo. 108 pp. London: Sidgwick and Jackson. 5s.

34. WYLD, H. C. K. A History of Modern Colloquial English. New York: E. P. Dutton & Co. [1920]. 23 cm. pp. xvi + 398. Rev. by H. M. Ayres in The Weekly Review, Oct. 27, 1920, III, 386–8, Times Lit. Suppl., July 1, 1920.

35. —— Kurze Geschichte des Englischen übersetzt von Heinrich Mutschmann. Heidelberg: Winter. 1919. pp. viii + 238. M. 5. Rev. Eilert Ekwall, Anglia, Beibl. 31, 177–185 (Aug. 1920).

IV. (c) ORTHOGRAPHY

36. GAAF, W. VAN DER. Notes on English Orthography (ie and ea). Neophilologus, V, 133, 333. 41 pp.

37. MATHESIUS, V. Filologické hlasy k opravě pravopisu Anglického. Philological opinions on English spelling reform. Naše Řeč, vol. 4, 1920. 129 n.

38. PERRETT, W. Peetickay: an Essay towards the Abolition of Spelling. 8vo. Cambridge: Heffer. 6s.

IV. (d) PHONOLOGY

39. ECKHARDT, E. Zur Quantität offener Tonvokale im Neuenglischen. Engl. Stud. 54, 117–132.

40. EHRENTREICH, A. Zur Quantität der Tonvokale im Modern-
Englischen (Auf Grund experimenteller Untersuchungen). Palaestra,
133 (Unters. u. Texte aus d. deutschen u. engl. Phil. her. v. Alois
Brandl, Gustav Roethe und Erich Schmidt). 1920. vii + 110 pp.,
mit 2 Tafeln. Berlin: Mayer und Müller. 15 Mk.

41. HOLTHAUSEN, F. Der Übergang von me. ne. -n zu m. Anglia,
Beibl. 31, 137–8.

42. HORN, W. Sprachgeschichtliche Bemerkungen (1. Ferndis-
similation und Fernassimilation. 2. Kontamination. 3. Über-
schriftsprachliche Formen). Engl. Stud. 54, 69–80.

43. JIRICZEK, O. L. Tenuis für Media im Altenglischen. Idg.
Forsch. 38, 196–199.

44. KELLER, W. Mittelenglische lange Vokale und die altfran-
zösische Quantität. Engl. Stud. 54, 111–117.

45. LUICK, K. Über Vokalverkürzung in abgeleiteten und zu-
sammengesetzten Wörtern. Engl. Stud. 54, 177–187.

46. WILSON, J. D. A Note on Elisions in 'The Faerie Queene.'
Mod. Lang. Rev. XV, 409–414.

IV. (e) INFLECTION AND WORD-FORMATION

47. DIETH, E. Flexivisches und Syntaktisches über das Pronomen
in der Ancren Riwle. Ein Beitrag zur mittelenglischen Syntax.
Zürich Diss. Zürich: Buchdruckerei Aschmann u. Scheller.

48. HÜBENER, G. Das Problem des Flexionsschwundes im Ags.
P. Br. B. 45, 85–102.

IV. (f) SYNTAX

49. BØGHOLM, N. English Prepositions. Kjøbenhavn og Christi-
ania, Gyldendalske Boghandel.

50. BOLKESTEIN, J. J. A. A special use of the Progressive Form.
De Drie Talen, Oct. 1920.

51. DARBY, Rev. A. The Mechanism of the Sentence. An Explanation of the Relations of Words in Organized Speech; for the
Use of Teachers of Language. New York. Oxford Univ. Press.

52. DEUTSCHBEIN, M. Die Einteilung der Aktionsarten. Engl.
Stud. 54, 80–87.

53. DIETH, E. Flexivisches und Syntaktisches. See IV, 47.

54. FIJN VAN DRAAT, P. The Article before Superlatives. Neophilologus, V, 348–51.

55. FRANZ, W. Grammatisches zu Shakespeare (I. Zur Inter-
punktion der Shakespeare-Folio von 1623. II. Der Satztypus: The
book sells well). Engl. Stud. 54, 132–139.

56. KENNEDY, A. G. The Modern English Verb-Adverb Combina-

8 BIBLIOGRAPHY

tion. Stanford Univ., Calif. 1920. Stanford University Publications: Language and Literature 1.

57. KIECKERS, E. Zur directen Rede im Neuenglischen. Engl. Stud. 53, 405–419.

58. KRUISINGA, E. Critical Contributions to English Syntax, in English Studies, vol. 2, No. 8, April 1920. pp. 40–7.

59. POUTSMA, H. Participles, The Syntax of, in English Studies, vol. 2, No. 7, February 1920. pp. 8–16.

60. —— The Subjunctive and Conditional in Principal Sentences, in De Drie Talen, Feb. and Mar. 1920.

61. —— The Subjunctive and the Conditional Mood in Modern English, in De Drie Talen, Apr. and May 1920.

62. —— The Subjunctive in Subordinate Questions. De Drie Talen, Nov. 1920.

63. VOLBEDA, R. What (a) en Such (a) voor abstracte zelfst. naamw. in Die Drie Talen, Aug.-Sept. 1920.

IV. (g) VULGAR ENGLISH, SLANG AND CANT

64. BRYAN, G. S. Cant in Language. Quart. Jour. Speech Education, June 1920, VI, 79–82.

65. BURTON, R. English as She is Spoke. The Bookman, July 1920, LI, 513–17.

66. DRENNAN, C. M. Cockney English and Kitchen Dutch. 8¼ × 5¼. Lecture delivered at University College, Johannesburg. Witwatersrand, Council of Education.

IV. (h) DIALECT

67. BRUNNER, K. Die Dialektliteratur von Lancashire. Wien, Verlag der Hochschule für Welthandel. 59 pp. 8°. 10 Kr.

68. GEPP, Rev. E. A Contribution to an Essex Dialect Dictionary. London: Routledge. 5s.

69. —— Supplement I. 8¼ × 5¼. Colchester: Benham. Rev. Times Lit. Suppl., June 17, 1920. 6d.

70. MOORMAN, F. W. Tales of the Ridings. With a Memoir of the Author by Professor C. Vaughan. Cr. 8vo. 7½ × 5. pp. 83. E. Mathews. 3s. 6d.

71. —— More Tales of the Ridings. Cr. 8vo. 7¾ × 5¼. pp. 84. 3s. 6d.

72. PARTINGTON, S. The Romance of Dialect. Middleton, Guardian Office. 2s. 6d. ('Much of his book consists of Middle English words which are still used in Lancashire.' Times Lit. Suppl., Sept. 16, 1920.)

73. WIEGERT, H. 'Jim an' Nell' von W. F. Rock. Eine Studie zum Dialekt von Devonshire. (Kap. 1–4.) Diss. Berlin. viii + 194 pp.

74. WYLD, H. C. South Eastern and South East Midland Dialects. (Essays and Studies by Members of the English Ass., vol. VI.) Oxford Univ. Press.

V. PHONETICS

1. ANNAKIN, M. L. Exercises in English Pronunciation. Halle: Niemeyer. 6 M.
2. BLANTON, S. and M. The Development of Speech Defects. In Quart. Jour. Speech Education, Feb. 1920, VI, 1, 33–43.
3. FRITZ, C. A. The Construction of the Organs of Speech and their Function in Speech Production. In Quart. Jour. Speech Education, Nov. 1920, VI, 4, 1–23. Illus.
4. GUNNISON, B. Oratoric Action. In Quart. Jour. Speech Education, Nov. 1920, VI, 4, 24–30.
5. JONES, D. Outline of English Phonetics. Reviewed by A. Schröer. Engl. Stud., Feb. 1920. pp. 419–430.
6. LEKY, M. Grundlagen einer allgemeinen Phonetik als Vorstufe zur Sprachwissenschaft. . Cologne: Bachem. 7 Mk.
7. LOUGHLIN, A. C. The Voice in Speaking and Singing. In Quart. Jour. Speech Education, Feb., Apr. 1920, VI, 1, 8–23, 2, 11–27.
8. MUCKEY, F. S. Sound Production in Speech. In Quart. Jour. Speech Education, June 1920, VI, 3, 54–8.
9. RICE, C. M. Charles Dickens, The Story of 'Our Mutual Friend.' Transcribed into Phonetic Notation, Part I. Cr. 8vo. 7¼ × 4¾. pp. 138. Cambridge: Heffer. 5s.
10. SCRIPTURE, E. W. Inscriptions of Speech. Reprints of Useful Knowledge, No. 308, from The Volta Review, July 1920. The Volta Bureau, Washington, D.C.
11. —— 1. Tracings from Speech Records. 2. The Organ of Voice. Reprint, No. 310, from The Volta Review, August 1920. The Volta Bureau, Washington, D.C. With excellent diagrams suitable for classes in Phonetics.
12. VIETOR, W. Kleine Phonetik des Deutschen, Englischen und Französischen. 11ᵉ Auflage. Reisland, Leipzig. 4.80 M.
13. WALLIS, G. The Philosophy of Speech. London: Allen & Unwin. 7s. 6d.
14. WOOLBERT, C. H. Speech and the Learning Process. In Quart. Jour. Speech Education, Feb. 1920, VI, 1, 55–75.
15. —— The Fundamentals of Speech. New York: Harper & Brothers. 1920. 21 cm. pp. xii + 384. Reviewed by A. T. W. in Quart. Jour. of Speech Education, Nov. 1920, VI, 4, 83–7.

VI. METRE AND STYLE

1. BAYFIELD, M. A. The Measures of the Poets: a New System of English Prosody. Cambridge Univ. Press. 1919. 21 cm. pp. vi [2], 112. Reviewed by J. R. Hulbert in Modern Philology, Jan. 1920, XVII, 727–9.
2. —— A Study of Shakespeare's Versification. With an enquiry into the trustworthiness of the early texts, an examination of the 1616 Folio of Ben Jonson's works and appendices, including a

revised text of Antony and Cleopatra. Cambridge Univ. Press. 16s.
Cf. The Plague of Elisions, Times Lit. Suppl., Feb. 26, 1920.

3. BESCHORNER, F. Verbale Reime bei Chaucer. Studien zur
englischen Philol. her. von Prof. L. Morsbach, Heft 60. vi + 32 pp.
Gr. 8°. Halle: Niemeyer. 5 Mk.

4. BRINK, A. Stab und Wort im Gawain, Eine stilistische Unter-
suchung, Morsbachs Studien für engl. Phil. Heft 59. 1920.
ix + 56 pp. Halle: Niemeyer. 10 Mk.

5. BRINK, B. TEN. Chaucer's Sprache und Verskunst. 3. Auflage
bearbeitet v. Ed. Eckhardt. 1920. xii + 243 pp. 8°. Leipzig: Chr.
Herm. Tauchnitz. 11 Mk.

6. BRUNNER, K. Die Reimsprache der sogen. Kentischen Fassung
der sieben weisen Meister. Archiv f. d. Stud. d. N. Spr. u. Lit. 140,
199–206.

7. —— Zum Balladenrhythmus. *Ib.* 140, 259–261.

8. CREEK, H. L. Rising and Falling Rhythm in English Verse.
Publications of the Modern Language Association of America, XXXV,
76–90, March 1920.

9. FIJN VAN DRAAT, P. The Place of the Adverb. A Study in
Rhythm. Neophilologus, vol. VI, 56–88.

10. FINSTERBUSCH, F. Der Versbau der mittelengl. Dichtungen Sir
Perceval of Galles und Sir Degrevant. (Wiener Beiträge zur Eng.
Phil. XLIX.) Vienna: C. Braumüller. 1920. 10 Mk.

11. FRANZ, W. Grammatisches (1. Absorption. 2. Prosarhythmus).
Germ. Rom. Mon. VIII, 250–2.

12. JACOB, C. F. The Foundations and Nature of Verse. New
York. Columbia University Press. 1918. 21 cm. pp. ix + 231.
Illus. (music). Reviewed by J. R. Hulbert in Modern Philology, Jan.
1920, XVII, 727–9; by Christian F. Ruckmich in Jour. Eng. and Germ.
Philol., July 1920, XIX, 430–33.

13. LEONARD, W. E. The Scansion of Middle English Alliterative
Verse. Studies by Members of the Dept. of English. Madison, Wis.
1920. Univ. of Wisconsin Studies in Lang. and Lit. 11.

14. MILLER, F. H. Stanzaic Division in York Play XXXIX. Mod.
Lang. Notes, 35–6, June 1920, pp. 379–380.

15. NEUNER, E. Über ein- und dreihebige Halbverse in der altenglischen alliterierenden Poesie. Berliner Diss. 1920. 87 pp. 5 Mk.

16. NIVEN, F. A Note upon Style. The Bookman, June 1920, LI,
434–7.

17. POUND, L. The 'Uniformity' of the Ballad Style. Mod. Lang.
Notes, 35, 4, April 1920, pp. 217–222.

18. SAINTSBURY, G. Some recent studies on English Prosody.
London. British Academy. 8vo. 1s. 6d.

19. SMITH, G. C. MOORE. The Use of an unstressed extra-metrical
syllable to carry the Rime. Mod. Lang. Rev., 15, 300–3, July 1920.

20. SNELL, A. L. F. An objective study of syllabic quantity in
English Verse. Pub. Mod. Lang. Ass. Amer. 34, 3 (1920).

21. SPIES, H. Alliteration und Reimklang im modernenglischen Kulturleben. Engl. Stud. 54, 149–159.
22. WILSON, J. D. A Note on Elisions in 'The Faerie Queene,' *see* IV, 46.

C. ENGLISH LITERATURE

VII. OLD ENGLISH

VII. (a) GENERAL

1. AMOS, FLORA ROSS. Early theories of translation. New York: Columbia University Press, 1920. 21 × 14½ cm. Theories of translation in English practice from the medieval period to Pope. Rev. Mod. Lang. Notes, XXXV, 380–384.
2. ARON, ALBERT WILLIAM. Traces of Matriarchy in Germanic Hero-Lore. Madison, Wis.: The Univ. of Wisconsin, 1920. 24·8 × 16·3 cm. pp. 77.
3. BALTENSBERGER, HERMANN. Eid, Versprechen und Treuschwur bei den Angelsachsen. Zürich Diss. Zürich: Buchdruckerei Aschmann u. Scheller.
4. BLOWS, S. Translation of Anglo-Saxon. For L.L.A. Examination in English Honours. With Vocabularies. Cr. 8vo. 7½ × 5. pp. 175. City of London Book Depot. 7s. 6d.
5. BROTANEK—EICHLER—SCHIPPER. Alt- und mittelenglisches Übungsbuch von Julius Zupitza. Wien u. Leipzig: Braumuller, 1915. Rev. by F. Holthausen, Anglia, Beibl. 31, 254–7.
6. IMELMANN, RUDOLF. Forschungen zur altenglischen Poesie (mit 2 Tafeln). In Commission bei der Weidmannschen Buchhandlung, Berlin, 1920. pp. 503.
7. KEISER, ALBERT. The Influence of Christianity on the Vocabulary of Old English Poetry. Urbana, Ill.: Univ. of Illinois, 1919–20. 27·5 cm. 2 vols. Univ. of Illinois Studies in Lang. and Lit. V, 1, 2. Rev. by Laurence Faucett in The Sewanee Rev., Oct.-Dec. 1920, XXVIII, 607–8.
8. NILSSON, M. P. Primitive Time Reckoning, translated from the Swedish. Roy. 8vo. Oxf. Univ. Press. 21s.
9. REEVES, WM PETERS. The Date of the Bewcastle Cross. Modern Language Notes, XXXV, 3, March 1920, pp. 155–160.
10. SARRAZIN, GR. Von Kädmon bis Kynewulf. Berlin: Mayer u. Müller. iii + 174 pp. 1913. Rev. by Georg Herzfeld. Anglia, Beibl. 31, 121–36. (Important.)
11. WEDEL, THEODORE OTTO. The Mediaeval Attitude toward Astrology, particularly in England. vi + 168pp. 22·5 × 14·5cm. New Haven: Yale University Press; London: Humphrey Milford, Oxford University Press. A Yale dissertation; LX Yale Studies in English.
12. WOLF, ALFRED. Die Bezeichnungen für Schicksal in der Angel-Sächsischen Poesie. 8vo. pp. 127. Breslau Diss.

VII. (b) OLD ENGLISH WRITINGS

Ælfred. 13. BROWNE, Right Rev. Bishop G. F. King Alfred's Books. London: S.P.C.K. 9¼ × 6¼. xxxii + 390 pp. 30s.

14. FARRER, WM. An Outline of Itinerary of King Alfred the First. Roy. 8vo. O.U.P. 18s.

15. JOST, KARL. Zur Textkritik der altengl. Soliloquienbearbeitung. Anglia, Beibl. 31, 259–272 u. 280–290.

Ælfric. 16. CRAWFORD, S. J. The Lincoln Fragment of the O.E. Version of the Heptateuch. Mod. Lang. Review, xv, 1–6, 1920.

17. LIEBERMANN, F. Ein staatsrechtlicher Satz Aelfrics aus lat. Quelle. Archiv f. d. St. d. N. Spr. u. Lit. 139, 84–5.

Beowulf. 18. ARON, ALBERT WILLIAM. Cf. VII, 2.

19. BJÖRKMANN, ERIK. Studien über die Eigennamen im Beowulf, Morsbachs Studien zur engl. Phil. Heft 58 (1920). xvii + 122 pp. Halle: Niemeyer. 12 Mk.

20. BRYAN, WILLIAM FRANK. Béowulf Notes. Journal of Eng. and Germanic Philol., Jan. 1920, XIX, 84–5.

21. HOOPS, JOHANNES. Das Verhüllen des Haupts bei Toten, ein angelsächsisch-nordischer Brauch (zu Beowulf 446: hafalan hydan). Engl. Stud. 54, 19–24.

22. HUBBARD, FRANK GAYLORD. The Plundering of the Hoard in Beowulf. In studies by members of the Dept. of English. Madison, Wis. 1920. Univ. of Wisconsin Studies in Language and Literature, 11.

23. LIEBERMANN, F. Ort und Zeit der Beowulfdichtung, Nachrichten der k. Gesellschaft der Wissenschaften zu Göttingen. Philologisch-Historische Klasse 1920. pp. 255–276.

24. RYPIUS, STANLEY I. The Beowulf Codex. In Modern Philology, Jan. 1920, XVII, 541–547.

25. SCHÜCKING, LEVIN L. Wiðergyld (Beowulf 2051). Engl. Stud. 53, 468–470.

26. THOMAS, W. Beowulf et les premiers fragments épiques anglosaxons. Étude critique et traduction. Paris: H. Didier. 2 fr. 50 c.

Caedmon. 27. BRADLEY, HENRY. The 'Caedmonian' Genesis (Engl. Ass. Essays and Studies, vol. VI). Oxford Univ. Press.

Cynewulf. 28. COOK, ALBERT STANBURROUGH, ed. The Old English Elene, Phœnix, and Physiologus. New Haven: Yale University Press, 1919. 21·5 × 15 cm. pp. lxxxix + 239 (1). Rev. by Howard R. Patch in Jour. Eng. and Germ. Philol., July 1920, XIX, 418–22; by J. W. B[right] in Mod. Lang. Notes, Apr. 1920, XXXV, 250–4.

29. HAMILTON, GEORGE LIVINGSTONE. The Sources of the Fates of the Apostles and Andreas. Modern Language Notes, XXXV, 7, November 1920, pp. 385–395. (To be continued in subsequent number.)

Early English Homilies. 30. FÖRSTER, MAX. Der Inhalt der altenglischen Handschrift Vespasianus D. XIV. Engl. Stud. 54, 46–69.

Glosses. 31. SCHLUTTER, O. B. Zu den Leidener Glossen. Anglia, 44, 386–388.

Indicia Monasterialia. 32. SWAEN, A. E. H. Note on the Anglo-Saxon Indicia Monasterialia. Archiv f. d. St. d. N. Spr. 140, 106 f.

Lyrics. 33. BRANDL, A. Venantius Fortunatus und die ags. Elegien 'Wanderer' und 'Ruine.' Archiv f. d. St. d. N. Spr. u. Lit. 139, 84.

Medicine. 34. SINGER, CHAS. Early English Magic and Medicine. British Academy. 8vo. O.U.P. 4s.

Phœnix. 35. COOK, ALBERT S. The Old English Elene, Phœnix and Physiologus. *See under* Cynewulf.

Physiologus. 36. COOK, ALBERT S. The Old English Elene, Phœnix and Physiologus. *See under* Cynewulf.

Psalter. 37. RAMSAY, ROBERT LEE. The Latin Text of the Paris Psalter: a Collation and Some Conclusions. In Am. Jour. Philology, April-June 1920, XLI, 147–76.

38. WILDHAGEN, KARL. Das Psalterium Gallicanum in England und seine altenglischen Glossierungen. Engl. Stud. 54, 35–46.

Riddles. 39. PATCH, HOWARD R. Anglo-Saxon Riddle 56. Modern Language Notes, XXXV, 3, March 1920, pp. 181–182.

Saints' Lives. 40. RYPINS, STANLEY I. The Old English Life of St Christopher. Modern Language Notes, XXXV, 3, March 1920, pp. 186–187.

Textual. 41. HOLTHAUSEN, F. Zum ae. Salomo und Saturn. Zur ae. Metrischen Psalmenübersetzung. Anglia, Beibl. 31, 190–198.

42. —— Zu altenglischen Dichtungen. Anglia, Beibl. 31, 25–32.

43. —— Zu den altenglischen Zaubersprüchen und Segen. Anglia, Beibl. 31, 116–120.

44. —— Zu altenglischen Dichtungen (1. Riddles, 2. Andreas, 3. Daniel, 4. Exodus, 5. Satan, 6. Verse of the Whale, 7. Later Genesis, 8. Cynewulf's Crist). Anglia, 44, 346–357.

45. KOCK, ERNST A. Jubilee Jaunts and Jottings. 250 Contributions to the Interpretation and Prosody of Old West Teutonic Alliterative Poetry. Lunds Universitets Årsskrift N. F. Avd. 1, Bd XIV, No. 26. Rev. by Fr. Klaeber in Jour. Eng. and Ger. Philol., July 1920, XIX, 409–13.

46. —— Interpretations and Emendations of Early English Texts VI and VII. Anglia, 44, 97–115 and 245–261.

Vision. 47. KONRATH, M. Eine altenglische Vision vom Jenseits. Archiv f. d. St. d. N. Spr. u. Lit. 139, 30–46.

Widsith. 48. JIRICZEK, O. L. Seafola im Widsith. Engl. Stud. 54, 15–19.

49. SCHÜTTE, GUDMUND. Vidsid og Slægtsagnene om Hengest og Angautyr. Arkiv f. Nord. Fil., N. F. 32, 1–32 (1920).

VIII. MIDDLE ENGLISH

VIII. (a) GENERAL

1. BASKERVILL, C. R. Dramatic Aspects of Mediæval Folk Festivals in England. Stud. in Phil. Univ. of N. Carolina, XVII, 1 (1920).

2. BROWN, CARLETON. A Register of Middle English Religious and Didactic Verse. Oxford: Printed for the Bibliographical Society at the Univ. Press. Vol. I, 1916. Vol. II, 1920. 22·4 × 18·6 cm. Part II reviewed by J. M. M[anley] in Modern Philology, Sept. 1920, XVIII, 287–8.

3. DEANESLY, MARGARET. Vernacular Books in England in the Fourteenth and Fifteenth Centuries. Modern Language Review, Oct. 1920.

4. HALL, JOSEPH. Selections from Early Middle English, 1130–1250. Oxford: Clarendon Press, 1920. 7½ × 5¼. Part I. Texts. viii + 222 pp. 7s. 6d. Part II. Notes. pp. 223–675. 15s.

5. HILKA, ALFONS. Zur Katharinen-legende: Die Quelle der Jugendgeschichte Katharinas. Archiv 140, 3 and 4 (1920).

6. JUSSERAND, J. J. English Wayfaring Life in the Middle Ages (XIVth Century). Transl. from the French by Lucy Toulmin Smith. New ed. Revised and enlarged by the Author. 9 × 6¼. pp. 464. London: Fisher Unwin. 25s.

7. LIEBERMANN, F. Zu Liedrefrain und Tanz im englischen Mittelalter. Archiv 140, 261–2.

8. —— (1) Zu Thomas Occleve; (2) Zu Chaucers Stellung in Hofämtern; (3) Zwischenspiele für Edward II. Archiv 140, 3 and 4 (1920).

9. SAVAGE, ERNEST A. A Monastic Humanist of the Fifteenth Century. The Library Association Record. June 1920. pp. 185–197.

10. WEDEL, T. O. The Medieval Attitude towards Astrology, particularly in England. (Yale Studies in English.) New Haven: Yale Univ. Press. London: Milford. 1920. 10s. 6d.

11. WESTON, JESSIE LAIDLAY. From Ritual to Romance. Cambridge University Press, 1920. XV + 202 pp. 23 cm. Reviewed by William A. Nitze in Modern Language Notes, XXXV, 6, June 1920, pp. 352–360.

11 a. —— Mystery Survivals in Medieval Romance. Quest. January 1920.

VIII. (b) MIDDLE ENGLISH WRITINGS

Ancren Riwle. 12. DIETH, EUGEN. Cf. IV, 47.

13. McNABB, VINCENT. Further Light on the Ancren Riwle. Mod. Lang. Rev. XV, 406–409. (*See* Hope Emily Allen, The Origin of the Ancren Riwle. Publ. Mod. Lang. Ass. Am. 33, 3, and G. G. Coulton's review in Mod. Lang. Rev. 15, 99–100.)

Arthurian Legend. 14. BROWN, ARTHUR CHARLES LEWIS. The Grail and the English Sir Perceval, XI. Modern Philology, August 1920, XVIII, 201–28.

15. HOLTHAUSEN, F. Zu Arthour and Merlin I. Anglia, Beibl. 31, 198–207.

16. MALORY, Sir THOMAS. Le Morte D'Arthur. (Biographical Note by A. W. Pollard.) Illustrated by Russell Flint. Medici Society, 1920. 9½ × 6¾. Vol. I. xxx + 439 pp. Vol. II. xxii + 531 pp. 42s.

17. —— Le Morte D'Arthur. Sir Thomas Malory's Book of King Arthur and of his Noble Knights of the Round Table. 2 vols. 9 × 6. pp. 467, 550. Macmillan. Each 7s. 6d.

Bible. 18. DEANESLY, MARGARET. The Lollard Bible and other Medieval Biblical Versions. 8vo. xv + 483 pp. Cambridge Univ. Press, 1920. 31s. 6d.

Caxton. 19. CAXTON. The Life of St George (from Caxton's Translation of the Golden Legend. Reprint). London: Alexander Moring. 8 × 5¾. 19 pp. 1s.

Chaucer. 20. BEATTY, JOSEPH M., Jr. A Companion of Chaucer. Modern Language Notes, XXXV, 4, April 1920, pp. 246–248. On Sir Robert de Assheton.

21. BESCHORNER, F. Verbale Reime bei Chaucer (Stud. zur engl. Phil. LVIII). Halle: M. Niemeyer, 1920. 5 Mk.

22. BLAU, E. Zu Chaucer's 'Tale of Sir Topas' ('payndemayn'). Anglia, Beibl. 31, 237.

23. BRINK, B. TEN. Chaucer's Sprache und Verskunst. See VI, 5.

24. BROWN, C. Mulier est hominis confusio (Chaucer's Nun's Priest's Tale). Mod. Lang. Notes, 35, 8, Dec. 1920.

25. CURRY, WALTER CLYDE. Chaucer's Reeve and Miller. Publications of the Modern Language Association of America, XXXV, 189–209, June 1920.

25a. —— The Secret of Chaucer's Pardoner. Journ. Eng. Germ. Phil. XXXVIII, 4 Oct. 1920.

26. DODD, WILLIAM GEORGE. Courtly Love in Chaucer and Gower. Harvard University Press. $2.50.

27. FARNHAM, WILLARD EDWARD. The Contending Lovers. Publications of the Modern Language Association of America, XXXV, 247–323, September 1920. Comparative study of a folk-lore theme, particularly in its oriental sources, though bearing specially on Chaucer's Parlement of Foules.

28. GRIM, FLORENCE M. Astronomical Lore in Chaucer. Lincoln, Neb. 1919. 8vo. pp. 96. University of Nebraska Studies in Language, Literature and Criticism 2. Reviewed by John S. P. Tatlock in Journal of Eng. and Germanic Philol., Jan. 1920, XIX, 129–30; by H. R. P. in Mod. Lang. Notes, Feb. 1920, XXXV, 128.

29. HOLTHAUSEN, F. Zu Chaucers 'Hous of fame.' Anglia, Beibl. 31, 137.

30. JACK, A. A. A Commentary on the Poetry of Chaucer and

Spenser. Glasgow: Maclehose and Jackson. Rev. Times Lit. Suppl., April 22, 1920. 8s. 6d.

31. KOCH, JOHN. Der Handschriftenverhältnis in Chaucers 'Legend of Good Women,' II. Anglia, 44, 23–72.

32. LANGE, HUGO. Die Legendenprologfrage. Zur Steuer der Wahrheit. Anglia, 44, 72–78. (Cf. V. Langhans, Anglia, Beibl. 31, 207 f.)

32a. —— Die Sonnen- und die Lilienstelle in Chaucers Legendenprolog. Ein neuer Beweis für die Priorität der F.-Redaction. Anglia, 44, 373–385.

32b. —— Zur Priorität des F.-Textes in Chaucers Legendenprolog und zur Interpretation von F. 531/2 = Gg. 519/20. Anglia, 44, 213–216.

33. LANGHANS, VICTOR. Chaucers Anelida and Arcite. Anglia, 44, 226–245. Id. Hugo Langes Artikel in Anglia (N.F. 32), 213. Anglia, 44 (N.F. 32), 337–345.

34. PATTERSON, R. F. Chaucer: Nonne Prest, His Tale. Ed. with Introduction and Notes. 18mo. Blackie. 2s.

35. RICKERT, EDITH. A New Interpretation of The Parlement of Foules. In Modern Philology, May 1920, XVIII, 1–29.

36. SHANNON, EDGAR FINLEY. Chaucer's Metamorphoseos. Modern Language Notes, XXXV, 5, May 1920, pp. 288–291.

37. STANFORD, MABEL A. The Sumner's Tale and St Patrick's Purgatory. In Jour. Eng. and Germ. Philology, July 1920, XIX, 377–81.

38. TATLOCK, JOHN S. P. Dante and Guinizelli in Chaucer's Troilus. Modern Language Notes, XXXV, 7, November 1920, p. 443.

Coventry Plays. 39. PATCH, HOWARD R. The Ludus Coventriae and the Digby Massacre. In Publications of the Modern Lang. Assn. of America, Sept. 1920, XXXV, 324–343.

Horn. 40. FUNKE, O. Zum Verkleidungsmotiv im King Horn. Anglia, Beibl. 31, 224.

Lollards. 41. SCHARPFF, PAULUS. Über ein englisches Auferstehungsspiel. Beitrag zur Geschichte des Dramas und der Lollarden. Erlanger Diss. 1919. 62 pp. 8°.

Mandeville. 42. HAMELIUS, P. Mandeville's Travels. Vol. 1. Text. E.E.T.S. Original Series, No. 153. 8vo. O.U.P. 15s.

Medicine. 43. HOLTHAUSEN, F. Zu den mittelenglischen medizinischen Gedichten. Anglia, 44, 357–373.

44. SCHÖFFLER, HERBERT. Beiträge zur mittelenglischen Medizinliteratur, I. Heft des sächsischen Forschungsinstituts in Leipzig für neuere Philologie. III. Angl. Abteilung. 1919. xv + 309 pp. Gr. 8°. Halle: M. Niemeyer. 20 Mk.

45. SINGER, CHAS. Early English Magic and Medicine. For The British Academy. 8vo. Oxford Univ. Press. 4s.

Minot, Lawrence. 46. MOORE, SAMUEL. Lawrence Minot. Modern Language Notes, XXXV, 2, February 1920, pp. 78–81.

The Owl and the Nightingale. 47. KENYON, JOHN SAMUEL. On the Date of the Owl and the Nightingale. In Modern Philology, May 1920, XVIII, 55–6.

Rolle, Richard of Hampole. 48. HULME, WILLIAM HENRY, ed. Richard Rolle of Hampole's Mending of Life. Ed. by William Henry Hulme. In Western Reserve Univ. Bulletins, N.S., XXI, 4, May 1918. Reviewed by M. Deanesly in Mod. Philology, Jan. 1920, XVII, 549–51.

Rule of St Benet. 49. HAGEL, FRIEDA. Zur Sprache der nord-englischen Prosaversion der Benediktiner-Regel. Anglia, 44, 1–23.

West Midland Poems. 50. BRINK, AUGUST. Stab und Wort im Gawain. See VI, 3.

51. JACKSON, T. Sir Gawain's Coat of Arms. Mod. Lang. Rev. 15, 77–79.

52. MENNEN, R. J. Purity: a Middle English Poem. Edited with Introduction, Notes, and Glossary by Robert J. Mennen. New Haven, Conn.: Yale Univ. Press. 1920. Yale Studies in English LXI.

53. SUNDÉN, K. F. Några förbisedda skand. lånord i Sir Gawayne, etc. Cf. III, 34.

54. TUTTLE, EDWIN H. Notes on the Pearl. Mod. Lang. Rev. XV, pp. 298–300.

Winner and Waster. 55. GOLLANCZ, Sir ISRAEL. A good short debate between Winner and Waster. (An alliterative poem on social and economic problems in England, 1382.) Select Early English Poems Series. London: H. Milford. 1920. 5s.

56. HULBERT, JAMES ROOT. The Problems of Authorship and Date of Wynnere and Wastoure. In Modern Philology, May 1920, XVIII, 31–40.

Miscellaneous. 57. HOLTHAUSEN, F. Das mittelengl. Streitgedicht 'The Eye and the Heart' (see E. Pr. Hammond's edition. Anglia, 34, 237 ff.). Anglia, 44, 85–94.

58. —— Zu mittelenglischen Dichtungen (Sir Degrevant, 519, 657; Sir Perceval, 687, 1876, 2279; Lydgate-Studien, Gedicht auf Mylady of Holand und Mylord of Gloucester). Anglia, 44, 78–85.

59. —— Ein mittelenglischer Hymnus auf Maria und Christus und seine Kymrische Umschrift. Archiv für d. Stud. d. n. Spr. 140, 33–43.

60. —— Weiteres zur Geschichte von Martin Waldeck. Zur Noah-Legende. Anglia Beibl. 31, 89–92.

VIII. (c) MIDDLE SCOTTISH

61. ROBB, T. D. Thre Prestis of Peblis. How thai told thar talis. Scottish Text Society. 1920.

62. SCHOFIELD, W. H. Mythical Bards and the Life of Wm Wallace. 8vo. Oxford Univ. Press. 12s. 6d.

63. SCHULTZ, JOHN RICHIE. Alexander Barclay and the Later Eclogue Writers. Modern Language Notes, XXXV, 1, January 1920, pp. 52–54.

64. WATT, LAUGHLAN MACLEAN. Douglas's Aeneid. 9¼ × 5¾.
xi + 252 pp. Cambridge: University Press. Rev. Times Lit. Suppl.
April 1, 1920. 14s.

IX. OLD AND MIDDLE ENGLISH: SUBSIDIARY

IX. (a) MYTHOLOGY, LEGEND, SAGA

1. GRÖNBECK, VILHELM. Vor Folkeæt i Oldtiden (I, Lykkemand
og Niding. II, Midgård og Menneskelivet. III, Hellighed og Hellig-
dom. IV, Menneskelivet og Guderne). Rev. by Eilert Ekwall, Anglia
Beibl. 31, 1–9 (important for O.E. heroic poetry).
2. HOLTHAUSEN, F. Ein lappisches Bärensohn-Märchen. Anglia
Beibl. 31, 66–67 (Beowulf).
3. —— Zur Vergleichenden Märchen- und Sagenkunde (2. Weiteres zur Geschichte von Martin Waldeck. 3. Zur Noah-Legende).
Anglia Beibl. 31, 89–92.
4. MARSTRANDER, C. Irske vidnesbyrd over Torsdyrkelse i Irland.
Nordisk Tidskrift för Filologi 1920, 1–2, pp. 8–32 (to be cont.).
5. NECKEL, GUSTAV. Sigmunds Drachenkampf. Edda, XIII, 1.
6. OLRIK, AXEL. The Heroic Legends of Denmark. Translated
from the Danish and revised in collaboration with the Author by
Lee M. Hollander. New York. The American-Scandinavian Founda-
tion. 1919. 24·5 cm. pp. xviii˙+ 530. Illus. Scandinavian Mono-
graphs iv. Rev. by William E. Mead in The Nation, Apr. 17, 1920,
CX, 520–1.

IX. (b) LEGAL AND HISTORICAL

7. SE BOYAR, GERALD E. Bartholomaeus Anglicus and His En-
cyclopaedia. In Journal of Eng. and Germanic Philol., April 1920,
XIX, 168–89.
8. BRAWLEY, BENJAMIN GRIFFITH. Wycliffe and the World War.
The Methodist Review, March-April 1920, CIII, 231–6.
9. DEANESLY, MARGARET. The Lollard Bible and other Medieval
Versions (Historical Background). See VIII, 18.
10. —— Vernacular Books in England in the Fourteenth and
Fifteenth Centuries. Mod. Lang. Rev. 1920, XV, 349–358.
11. KINGSFORD, CHARLES LETHFORD, F.S.A. The Stonor Letters
and Papers, 1290–1483 (Royal Historical Society: Camden Third
Series). Rev. Times Lit. Suppl., Feb. 24, 1921.
12. KRUISINGA, E. A History of English Law Courts, in English
Studies, vol. 2, No. 11, Oct. 1920, pp. 131–5.
13. PARRY, A. W. Education in England in the Middle Ages.
London D.Sc. Thesis. Univ. Tutorial Press. 7s. 6d.
14. WALBERG, EMANUEL. När författades Wilhelm av Canter-
burys Miracula Sancti Thomæ Cantuariensis? Studier i Modern

Språkvetenskap utg. av Nyfilologiska Sällskapet, Stockholm, vii, 1920. pp. 14.

15. WILSON, Rev. JAMES M. The Worcester Liber Albus. Glimpses of Life in a great Benedictine Monastery in the 14th Century. 8vo. 8¾ × 5½. pp. 302. S.P.C.K. 15s.

X. MODERN ENGLISH

1. SIXTEENTH CENTURY

(a) GENERAL

1. BAYFIELD, M. A. Elizabethan Printing: An instructive Blunder. Times Lit. Suppl. 23 Sept. 1920.

2. BEACH, SARAH MOREHOUSE. The 'Julius Cæsar Obelisk' in the English Faust Book and Elsewhere. Modern Language Notes, xxxv, 1, January 1920, pp. 27–31.

3. BERDAN, JOHN M. Studies in Tudor Literature: Early Tudor Poetry, 1485–1547. New York: Macmillan. 22·3 × 16 cm. pp. xix, [3], 564.

4. CRANE, THOMAS FREDERICK. Italian Social Customs of the Sixteenth Century and their Influence on the Literatures of Europe. New Haven: Yale Univ. Press. 24 × 16 cm. pp. xv + 689. Cornell Studies in English v.

5. FELLOWES, E. H. (ed. by). English Madrigal Verse, 1588–1632. Edited from the original song-books. Oxford: Clarendon Press. London: Milford. xx + 640 pp. 12s. 6d.

6. GREENLAW, EDWIN, and MOFFATT, JAMES STRONG. Recent Literature [on the Elizabethan Period]. In Studies in Philology, April 1920, xvii, 246–68. Many annotations.

7. LAWRENCE, W. J. The Authorship of 'Fedele and Fortunio.' Times Lit. Suppl. May 20, 1920. Cf. F. S. Boas, Feb. 20, 1919.

8. MUSS-ARNOLT, WILLIAM. The Scottish Service Book of 1637 and Its Successors: a Bio-Bibliographical Study. In Amer. Jour. of Theology, July 1920, xxiv, 386–406.

9. REYNOLDS, MYRA. The Learned Lady in England, 1650–1760. Vassar Semi-Centennial Series. Boston: Houghton, Mifflin Co. $2.25.

10. ROLLINS, H. E. (ed. by). Old English Ballads, 1553–1623. Cambridge: University Press. 9 × 6. xxxi + 423 pp. 18s. 6d.

11. TAYLOR, HENRY OSBORN. Thought and Expression in the Sixteenth Century. New York: Macmillan. 2 vols. 22·5 cm.

12. ZEITLIN, JACOB. Commonplaces in Elizabethan Life and Letters. In Journal of Eng. and Germanic Philol., January 1920, xix, 47–65.

(b) AUTHORS

Bacon, Francis. 13. TALLADA, J. M. Study on the Communistic Utopy 'Nova Atlantis.' (Catalan.) La Rivista, 1920, p. 234.

14. WOODWARD, PARKER. Sir Francis Bacon: Poet, philosopher, statesman, lawyer, wit. 8vo. 9 × 5¾. x + 157 pp. London: Grafton. 10s. 6d.

Coventry Plays. 15. PATCH, HOWARD ROLLIN. The Ludus Coventriae and the Digby Massacre. In Publ. Mod. Lang. Ass. America, Sept. 1920, XXXV, 324–43.

Drayton, Michael. 16. SCHAUBERT, E. VON. Draytons Anteil an Heinrich VI, 2. und 3. Teil. *See* Shakespeare.

Elderton, William. 17. ROLLINS, HYDER EDWARD. William Elderton: Elizabethan Actor and Ballad-Writer. In Studies in Philology, April 1920, XVII, 199–245.

Eliot, Thomas. 18. SCHRÖDER, K. Platonismus in der englischen Renaissance vor und bei Thomas Eliot nebst Neudruck von Eliots 'Disputation Platonike,' 1533. Palæstra 95. 8vo. x + 153, 107. Berlin: Meyer und Müller. 28 M.

Gammer Gurton's Nedle. 19. BRETT-SMITH, H. F. B. (ed. by). Gammer Gurton's Nedle. By Mr S. Mr of Art (The Percy Reprints, No. 2). Cr. 8vo. 7¾ × 5¼. xv + 80 pp. Oxford: Blackwell. 4s. 6d.

Greene, Robert. 20. McCALLUM, JAMES DOW. Greene's Friar Bacon and Friar Bungay. Modern Language Notes, XXXV, 4, April 1920, pp. 212–217.

Heywood, Jasper. 21. FISCHER, WALTHER. Zur Biographie Kaspar Heywoods. Engl. Stud. 54, 352–358.

J. M. gent. 22. LYON, J. H. H. A Study of 'The New Metamorphosis' written by J. M. gent., 1600. New York: Columbia Univ. Press. London: Milford. 8s. 6d.

More, Sir Thomas. 23. DALY, JAMES J. Sir Thomas More, Saint and Humorist. In The Catholic World, July 1920, CXI, 463–70.

24. HUGHES, MERRITT T. Spenser and Utopia. In Studies in Philology, April 1920, XVII, 132–146.

Nashe, Thomas. 25. BRETT-SMITH, H. F. B. (ed. by). 'The Unfortunate Traveller or the Life of Jack Wilton,' by Thomas Nashe. Oxford: Blackwell. Rev. Times Lit. Suppl. April 15, 1920. 5s.

Nevile, Alexander. 26. SPEARING, E. M. Alexander Nevile's Translation of Seneca's 'Oedipus.' Modern Language Review, Oct. 1920.

Peele, George. 27. BATES, KATHARINE LEE. The Date of Peele's Death. Modern Language Notes, XXXV, 1, January 1920, p. 54. Note.—Only brief note of 11 lines giving evidence that Peele died November 9, 1596.

Raleigh, Sir Walter. 28. ANDREWS, CHARLES M. Raleigh's Place in American Colonization. Columbia University Dissertation.

The Shepherd Tony. 29 BYRNE, M. ST CLAIRE. The Shepherd Tony. A Recapitulation. Mod. Lang. Review, Oct. 1920.

Spenser, Edmund. 30. BASKERVILL, CHARLES READ. The Genesis of Spenser's Queen of Faerie. In Modern Philology, May 1920, XVIII, 49–54.

31. CORY, HERBERT ELLSWORTH. Edmund Spenser. A Critical Study. By Herbert Ellsworth Cory. Berkeley: University of California Press. 1917. viii + 478 pp. Univ. of California Publ., Modern Philology v. Reviewed by Edwin Greenlaw in Modern Language Notes, March 1920, XXXV, 165–177.

32. COULTER, CORNELIA CATLIN. Two of E. K.'s Classical Allusions. Modern Language Notes, XXXV, 1, January 1920, pp. 55–56.

33. DODGE, R. E. NEIL. Spenser's Imitations from Ariosto—Addenda. Publications of the Modern Language Association of America, XXXV, 91–92, March 1920.

34. GREENLAW, EDWIN. Spenser and Lucretius. In Studies in Philology, October 1920, XVII, 439–64.

34a. —— Spenser's Influence on Paradise Lost. In Studies in Philology, July 1920, XVII, 320–59.

35. HUGHES, MERRITT T. Spenser and Utopia. In Studies in Philology, April 1920, XVII, 132–46.

36. JACK, A. A. 'Commentary on the Poetry of Chaucer and Spenser.' Glasgow: Maclehose, Jackson & Co. 1920. 7¾ × 5¼. xi + 369 pp. 8s. 6d.

37. JONES, HARRIE STUART VEDDER. Spenser's Defense of Lord Grey. Urbana, Ill. The University of Illinois. 1919. 27·9 × 18 cm. pp. 75. Univ. of Illinois Studies, v, 3. Rev. by Preserved Smith in The Nation, Apr. 24, 1920, CX, 555.

38. MUSTARD, WILFRED PIRT. Notes on The Shepheardes Calender. Modern Language Notes, XXXV, 6, June 1920, pp. 371–372.

39. OSGOOD, CHARLES GROSVENOR. Spenser's English Rivers. In Trans. Connecticut Academy of Arts and Sciences, Jan. 1920, XXIII, 65–108.

39a. —— The 'Doleful Lay of Ciorinda.' Modern Language Notes, XXXV, 2, February 1920, pp. 90–96.

40. Spenser's Faerie Queene. Book VII, Canto vii. With Introduction and notes. (April 1920.) pp. 72. 8vo. 1st ed. Printers: K. Sakalagunam Nāyudu, British Press, Madras. Price, 10 annas.

41. WHITMAN, CHARLES HUNTINGTON. A Subject-Index to the Poems of Edmund Spenser. New Haven: Yale Univ. Press. 1918. 24 cm. pp. xi + 261. Reviewed by C. R. B[askervill] in Modern Philology, Jan. 1920, XVII, 552; in The Nation, Feb. 14, 1920, CX, 209.

Surrey, Henry Howard, Earl of. 42. PADELFORD, FREDERICK MORGAN. The Poems of Henry Howard, Earl of Surrey. Seattle: The University of Washington. 1920. Univ. of Washington: Publications in Language and Literature, vol. 1.

Surrey. 43. WILLCOCK, GLADYS D. A Hitherto Uncollated Version of Surrey's Translation of the Fourth Book of the 'Aeneid.' II. Mod. Lang. Review, April 1920.

2. SEVENTEENTH CENTURY

(a) GENERAL

44. ALDEN, RAYMOND MACDONALD. The Lyrical Conceits of the Metaphysical Poets. In Studies in Philology, April 1920, XVII, 183–98.

45. BOAS, F. S. Stage Censorship under Charles II. Times Literary Supplement, April 15, 22, 1920.

46. BROWN, CARLETON. The Stonyhurst Pageants. 9¼ × 6¼. 30 + 302 pp. Baltimore: The Johns Hopkins Press. 1920. 8s. 6d. (17th c. Miracle Plays.)

47. CLOUGH, BEN C. Notes on the Metaphysical Poets. Modern Language Notes, XXXV, 2, February 1920, pp. 115–117.

48. DOBELL, P. J. Books of the Time of the Restoration, being a collection of Plays, Poems and Prose Works, described and annotated. London: Dobell. 6s.

49. MASSINGHAM, HAROLD JOHN, ed. A Treasury of Seventeenth Century English Verse from the Death of Shakespeare to the Restoration (1616–1660). London: Macmillan. 1919. 16 cm. pp. xxiii + 399. Front. (port.). Rev. in The Nation, Jan. 31, 1920, CX, 151.

50. PARKER, KARL THEODOR. Oliver Cromwell in der schönen Literatur Englands. Eine literarische Studie. Zürcher Dissertation. Speyer und Kärner, Universitätsbuchhandlung, Freiburg i. B.

51. PARRY, JOHN J. A Seventeenth Century Gallery of Poets. In Jour. Eng. and Germanic Philol., April 1920, XIX, 270–77.

52. REYNOLDS, MYRA. The Learned Lady in England, 1650–1760. Boston: Houghton, Mifflin Co. 1920. 23 cm. pp. [xii], 489, [1]. Front. plates, ports. Vassar Semi-Centennial Ser. Bibliography, pp. [459]–476.

53. SCHAFER, ROBERT. The English Ode and 1660. An Essay in Literary History. Princeton Diss. 9 × 6, vi + 167 pp. Princeton: Univ. Press. London: Milford.

54. WRIGHT, THOMAS GODDARD, Literary Culture in Early New England, 1620–1730. New Haven: Yale University Press.

(b) AUTHORS

Alexander, Sir William, Earl of Stirling. 55. KASTNER, L. E. and CHARLTON, H. B. The Poetical Works of Sir William Alexander Earl of Stirling. Vol. 1. The Dramatic Works. Manchester Univ. Press. London: Longmans. Rev. Times Lit. Suppl. Feb. 24, 1921. 28s.

Carleton, Mary. 56. BERNBAUM, E. The Mary Carleton Narratives, 1663–1673. A missing chapter in the history of the English Novel. 106 pp. London: Milford. 5s. 6d.

Chamberlain, John. 57. STATHAM, EDWARD PHILLIPS. A Jacobean Letter writer—the Life and Times of John Chamberlain. 9 × 5¾. xvi + 248 pp. London: Kegan Paul. 12s. 6d.

Cowley, Abraham. 58. BELLOT, H. H. Abraham Cowley. Nineteenth Cent., Sept. 1920.

Donne, John. 59. ARONSTEIN, PH. John Donne als Dichter. Ein Beitrag zur Kenntnis d. englischen Renaissance (101 pp.). Gr. 8°. Halle, 1920. (Offprint from Anglia, 44, 115–213.) 12 Mk.

60. Sermons: Selected Passages. With an Essay by Logan Pearsall Smith. Oxford: The Clarendon Press. 19·5 cm. pp. lii + 263, [1]. Rev. in The Nation, Jan. 17, 1920, cx, 79–80.

61. SMITH, G. C. MOORE. Izaak Walton and John Donne. Mod. Lang. Rev. xv, 303. (Identification of Walton's 'ingenuous and learned man.')

Drummond, William of Hawthornden. 62. CLEGG, SAMUEL (ed. by). William Drummond of Hawthornden: 'A Cypress grove.' With Introduction and Notes. 8vo. 8¾ × 5½. pp. 78. Hawthornden Press, C. J. Sawyer. 6s. 6d.

Dryden, John. 63. VAN DOREN, MARK. The Poetry of John Dryden. New York: Harcourt, Brace and Howe. 1920. Reviewed by Stuart P. Sherman in The Nation, Dec. 1, 1920, cxi, 619–20.

Herbert, George (1593–1630). 64. PALMER, GEORGE HERBERT. The English Works of George Herbert. Newly arranged and annotated and considered in relation to his life. Houghton, Mifflin Co. Rev. Times Lit. Suppl., April 1, 1920. 50s.

Jonson, Ben. 65. DRAPER, JOHN W. A Reference to 'Huon' in Ben Jonson. Modern Language Notes, xxxv, 7, November 1920, pp. 439–440.

66. HARRIS, LYNN H. Three Notes on Ben Jonson. In Modern Philology, January 1920, xvii, 679–85.

67. LAWRENCE, W. J. The Casting-out of Ben Jonson. Times Literary Supplement, July 8, 1920.

Locke. 68. TAGLIATETA, E. Giovanni Locke educatore. Roma: Signorelli.

Marston, John. 69. ALLEN, MORSE SHEPARD. The Satire of John Marston. Princeton Univ. Diss. Columbus, Ohio: F. J. Heer Printing Co. 1920. 22·5 cm. pp. [ii], 187.

Milton, John. 70. BALDWIN, EDWARD CHAUNCEY. Milton and Plato's Timæus. Publications of the Modern Language Association of America, xxxv, 210–217, June 1920.

71. GILBERT, ALLAN H. A Geographical Dictionary of Milton. New Haven, Conn.: Yale University Press. 1918. 24 × 16 cm. pp. viii + 322. Cornell Studies in English iv. Reviewed by G. S. in Modern Philology, Jan. 1920, xvii, 551–2.

72. —— Milton and the Mysteries. In Studies in Philology, Apr. 1920, xvii, 147–69.

72 *a*. GILBERT, ALLAN H. Milton on the Position of Woman. I, II. Mod. Lang. Review, Jan., July, 1920.

73. GLICKSMAN, HARRY. Lowell on Milton's Areopagitica. Modern Language Notes, xxxv, 3, March 1920, pp. 185–186.

73 *a*. —— The Editions of Milton's History of Britain. Publications of the Modern Language Association of America, xxxv, 116–122, March 1920.

73 *b*. —— The Sources of Milton's History of Britain. In Studies by Members of the Dept. of English. Madison, Wis. 1920. Univ. of Wisconsin Studies in Lang. and Lit. 11.

74. GREENLAW, EDWIN. Spenser's Influence on Paradise Lost. In Studies in Philology, July 1920, xvii, 320–59.

75. HALLER, WILLIAM. Order and Progress in Paradise Lost. Publications of the Modern Language Association of America, 218–225, June 1920.

76. HANFORD, JAMES HOLLY. The Date of Milton's De Doctrina Christiana. In Studies in Philology, July 1920, xvii, 309–19.

77. HIMES, JOHN A. Some Interpretations of Milton. Modern Language Notes, xxxv, 7, November 1920, pp. 441–442.

78. HÜBENER, GUSTAV. Milton—der Albino. Engl. Stud. 54, 473–77.

79. LILJEGREN, S. B. Bemerkungen zur Biographie Miltons. Engl. Stud. 54, 358–367.

80. LINDELÖF, U. Milton Biografier, 9. 112 pp. Helger Schildts, Helsingfors. 12 Mark.

81. MUTSCHMANN, HEINRICH. Milton und das Licht. Die Geschichte einer Seelenerkrankung. Sonderdruck aus Anglia Beibl. 30. Bd. 1920, vi + 76 pp. Gr. 8°. Halle: M. Niemeyer. 2.80 Mk.

81 *a*. —— Der andere Milton. xii + 112 pp. Gr. 8°. Bonn: K. Schroeder. 5 Mk.

82. OSGOOD, CHARLES GROSVENOR. Paradise Lost, 9, 506; Nativity Hymn 133–153. In American Jour. of Philol., Jan.-March 1920, xli, 76–80.

83. SAURAT, DENIS. Blake and Milton. 74 pp. 16·5 × 25. Alcan, Paris. (Petite these.) 7 f. 50.

84. —— La pensée de Milton. 770 pp. 16·5 × 25. Alcan, Paris. (Grande thèse.) 20 f.

85. SHERBURN, GEORGE. The Early Popularity of Milton's Minor Poems. In Modern Philology, September 1919, January 1920, xvii, 259–78, 515–40.

86. THALER, ALWIN. Milton in the Theatre. In Studies in Philology, July 1920, xvii, 269–308.

87. TUPPER, JAMES WADDELL. The Dramatic Structure of Samson Agonistes. Publications of the Modern Language Association of America, xxxv, 375–389, September 1920.

Pepys, Samuel. 88. TANNER, J. R. Samuel Pepys and the Royal Navy. (Lees Knowles Lectures. Trin. Coll. Cam.) Cambridge Univ. Press. 1920. 6s. 6d.

89. WARSHAW, JACOB. Pepys as a Dramatic Critic. In The Drama, March-April 1920, X, 209–13.

3. EIGHTEENTH CENTURY

(a) GENERAL

90. AMOS, FLORA ROSS. Early Theories of Translation. New York: Columbia Univ. Press. 1920. 21 × 14½ cm. Theories of Translation in English practice from the Medieval Period to Pope. Rev. Mod. Lang. Notes, 35, 380–388.

91. COLVILLE, K. N. A Miscellany of the Wits. Select pieces by William King D.C.L., John Arbuthnot M.D. and other Hands. With an Introduction. Rev. Times Lit. Suppl. Jan. 20, 1921. Philip Allen. 15s.

92. FRAZER, Sir JAMES G. Sir Roger de Coverley and other Literary Pieces. 7¾ × 5¼. xii + 319 pp. London: Macmillan & Co. 1920. 8s. 6d.

93. KALKÜHLER, FLORINE. Die Natur des Spleens bei dem englischen Schriftstellern in der 1. Hälfte des 18. Jahrhunderts. Borna, Leipzig. 1920. viii + 46. 8°. Münster Diss.

94. MORE, PAUL ELMER. With the Wits. Shelburne Essays. Tenth Series. Boston: Houghton, Mifflin Co. 1919. 19·5 cm. pp. xii, [2], 311, [1]. Beaumont and Fletcher. Halifax. A Bluestocking of the Restoration [Aphra Behn]. Swift. Pope. Lady Mary Wortley Montagu. A Philosopher Among the Wits [Bishop Berkeley]. A Duke Among the Wits [Duke of Wharton]. Gray's Letters. Decadent Wit. Index to Shelburne Essays. Rev. by Stuart P. Sherman in The Review, Jan. 17, 1920, II, 54–6. Times Lit. Suppl., May 20th.

95. PATTON, JULIA. The English Village: a Literary Study, 1750–1850. New York: The Macmillan Company. 1919. 19½ cm. pp. xii + 236. Reviewed by Leslie N. Broughton in Journal of Eng. and Germanic Philol., Jan. 1920, XIX, 125–8.

(b) AUTHORS

Addison, Joseph. 96. O'CONNOR, HORACE W. Addison in Young's Conjectures. Modern Language Notes, XXXV, 1, January 1920, pp. 24–26.

Blake, William. 97. FEHR, BERNHARD. William Blake und die Kabbala. Engl. Stud. 54, 139–149.

98. GARDNER, CHARLES. William Blake, the Man. New York: E. P. Dutton & Co. 1919. 21·5 cm. pp. 202, [1]. Front., plates, port. Rev. in The Review, Feb. 21, 1920, II, 181–2.

99. SAURAT, DENIS. Blake and Milton. *See* Milton.

Burns, Robert. 100. LAYDEN, FRANKLYN BLISS. Notes on Burns and Thomson. In Jour. Eng. and Germ. Philol., July 1920, XIX, 305–17.

Churchill, Charles. 101. BEATTY, JOSEPH M., jr. An Essay in Critical Biography—Charles Churchill. Publications of the Modern Language Association of America, 226–246, June 1920.

Cumberland, Richard. 102. WILLIAMS, S. T. Richard Cumberland's 'West Indian.' Mod. Lang. Notes, 35, 7 (Nov.).

Defoe, Daniel. 103. De Foe. Les pirateries du Capitaine Singleton. 12 × 19. Anon. trad. Edit. fr. ill. Paris. 5 f. 50.

104. BOREL, PETRUS, trad. La Vie et les Aventures étranges et surprenantes de Robinson Crusoe. 2 vols. 320 + 306 pp. 14·5 × 22·5. Soc. litt. de Fr. Paris. 40 f.

105. FERNSEMER, O. F. W. Daniel Defoe and the Palatine Emigration of 1709: a New View of the Origin of Robinson Crusoe. In Journal of Eng. and Germanic Philol., Jan. 1920, XIX, 94–124.

106. FREEMAN, LEWIS R. Where is Robinson Crusoe's Island? In Travel, Feb. 1920, XXXIV, 27–30. Illus., map.

107. HÜBENER, GUSTAV. Der Kaufmann Robinson Crusoe. Engl. Stud. 54, 367–399.

108. LÜTHI, ALBERT. Daniel Defoe und seine Fortsetzungen zu Robinson Crusoe. Zürcher Dissertation. Stuttgart: Druck der Aktiengesellschaft Deutsches Volksblatt. 1920.

109. NICHOLSON, WATSON. The Historical Sources of Defoe's Journal of the Plague Year. 7¾ × 5¼. 182 pp. Boston, U.S.A.: The Stratford Co. 1920. $2.

Evelyn, John. 110. MAYNARD SMITH, H. The early Life and Education of John Evelyn. With a Commentary. (Oxford Historical and Liter. Studies.) Oxford: Clar. Press. 12s. 6d.

Fielding, Henry. 111. DIGEON, A. Autour de Fielding: Miss Fielding, son frère, et Richardson; Fielding, conseiller littéraire de sa sœur, est portraituré par elle. (2 art.) Revue Germanique Nos. 3 et 4. pp. 209–219 et 353–362.

Godwin, William. 112. ALLEN, BEVERLY SPRAGUE. William Godwin and the Stage. In Publ. Mod. Lang. Assn America, Sept. 1920, XXXV, 358–74.

Goldsmith, Oliver. 113. FARRAN Y MAYORAL, J. Oliver Goldsmith 'El Vicari de Wakefield.' Editorial Catalana. 8vo. pp. 212. (Biblioteca literària.) Rev. La Revista, 1920, p. 59.

Gray, Thomas. 114. CLOUGH, BEN C. Full Many a Gem. Modern Language Notes, XXXV, 2, February 1920, p. 117. Note.—A brief note giving a possible source of Gray's line in the Iter Boreale of R. Wild, D.D. (1671).

115. DEL RE, ARUNDEL. Gray and Cambridge in 1769. Times Lit. Suppl., Sept. 23, 1920. Extract from de Bonstetten's 'Souvenirs écrites en 1831.'

116. SARGEAUNT, J. The Text of Walpole's and Gray's Letters. Times Lit. Suppl., May 13, 1920.

Johnson, James, †1811. 117. SCHWEBS, E. Schottische Volkslyrik in James Johnson's 'The Scots' Musical Museum.' Palæstra 95. Berlin: Mayer und Müller. 20 Mk.

Johnson, Samuel. 118. GILCHRIST, MARIE EMILLE. A Dictionary to Read: Johnson's Dictionary. In Poet Lore, June 1920, XXXI, 291–6.

119. Johnson Club Papers, by various hands. 2nd series. 7¾ × 5½. 238 pp. London: Fisher Unwin. 1920. 10s. 6d.

120. WHITFORD, ROBERT CALVIN. Lexiphanes: Satire's View of Doctor Johnson. In The So. Atlantic Quarterly, Apr. 1920, XIX, 141–56.

Macpherson, James. 121. MALMSTEDT, A. Ossian. Studier i Modern Språkvetenskap utg. av Nyfilologiska Sällskapet, Stockholm, VII, 1920. pp. 36.

122. VAN TIEGHEM, F. Ossian et l'Ossianisme dans la littérature européenne au XVIIIᵉ siècle. (In Neophilologische Bibliothek.) 60 pp. 24 × 15 cm. Groningen: J. B. Wolters. Fl. 2.40.

Osborne, Dorothy. 123. SMITH, G. C. MOORE. Dorothy Osborne's Letters. Notes and Queries, Sept. 25—Nov. 13, 1920.

123a. —— New Light on Dorothy Osborne's Letters. Times Lit. Suppl., 23 Sept., 28 Oct.

Pepys, Samuel. 124. TANNER, J. R. Pepys (Samuel) and the Royal Navy. (Lees Knowles Lectures, 1919, Cambridge.) 8vo. 9 × 5¾. pp. 83. Cambridge Univ. Press, 1920. 6s. 6d.

Percy, Thomas, Bishop of Dromore. 125. RINAKER, CLARISSA. Percy as a Sonneteer. Modern Language Notes, XXXV, 1, January 1920, pp. 56–58.

Pope, Alexander. 126. CRAWFORD, R. A Portrait of Alexander Pope. Library, I, 2. Sept.

127. JONES, RICHARD F. Another of Pope's Schemes. Modern Language Notes, XXXV, 6, June 1920, pp. 346–351.

128. MACKAIL, JOHN WILLIAM. Pope. Cambridge: Univ. Press. 1919. 19 cm. pp. 47, [1]. The Leslie Stephen Lecture, 1919. Rev. in The Nation, Jan. 17, 1920, CX, 79.

Shenstone, William. 129. HAZELTINE, ALICE ISABEL. A Study of William Shenstone and of His Critics, with Fifteen of His Unpublished Poems and Five of His Unpublished Latin Inscriptions. Menasha, Wis.: Geo. Banta. 1918. 23½ cm. pp. vi + 94. Reviewed by G. S. in Modern Philology, Jan. 1920, XVII, 183.

Sterne, Laurence. 130. PINGER, W. R. R. Laurence Sterne and Goethe. Berkeley, Calif.: Univ. of California Press. 1920. Univ. of California Publ. in Modern Philology, X, 1, pp. 1–65.

131. RABIZZANI, G. Sterne in Italia. Roma: Formiggini.

Swift, Jonathan. 132. BRÉGY, KATHERINE MARIE CORNELIA. The Enigma of Dean Swift. In The Catholic World, Oct. 1920, CXII, 52–9.

133. ELDER, LUCIUS W. The Pride of the Yahoo. Modern Lan
guage Notes, XXXV, 4, April 1920, pp. 206–211.

134. FIRTH, C. H. The Political Significance of Gulliver's Travels.
For the British Academy. 23 pp. London: Milford. 1920. 1s. 6d.

135. GUTHKELCH, A. C. and SMITH, D. NICHOL (ed. by). 'A Tale
of a Tub,' to which is added 'The Battle of the Books and the Mechan-
ical Operation of the Spirit,' by Jonathan Swift, together with 'The
History of Martin,' Wotton's observations upon the Tale of a Tub,
Curll's complete key, etc. The whole edited with an Introduction and
Notes, historical and explanatory. Oxford: Clarendon Press. 1920.
24s.

136. JONES, RICHARD F. The Background of The Battle of the
Books, 1920. Reprinted from Washington University Studies, VII,
Humanistic Series 2.

Theobald, Lewis. 137. JONES, RICHARD FOSTER. Lewis Theobald:
His Contribution to English Scholarship. With Some Unpublished
Letters. New York: Columbia University Press. 1919. 21 cm. pp.
xi + 363. Columbia Univ. Studies in Eng. and Comparative Liter-
ature. Reviewed by George Sherburn in Modern Philology, May 1920,
XVIII, 57–63.

Thomson, James. 138. SNYDER, FRANKLYN BLISS. Notes on
Burns and Thomson. In Jour. Eng. and Germ. Philol., July 1920,
XIX, 305–17.

Walpole, Horace. 139. FINCH, M. B. and E. ALLISON PEERS.
Walpole's Relations with Voltaire. In Modern Philology, August
1920, XVIII, 189–200.

140. SARGEAUNT, J. The Text of Walpole's and Gray's Letters.
Times Literary Suppl., May 13, 1920.

Webb, Daniel. 141. HECHT, HANS. Daniel Webb. Ein Beitrag zur
englischen Aesthetik des 18. Jahrh. Mit einem Abdruck der Remarks
on the beauties of poetry 1762 und einem Titelkupfer, 1920. iii + 117
pp. 8°. Hamburg: H. Grand. 10 Mk.

Wesley, John. 142. GILLIES, ANDREW. Sidelights on John Wesley
from Boswell's Johnson. In The Methodist Review, Jan.-Feb. 1920,
CIII, 22–9.

Young, Edward. 143. MORLEY, EDITH J. Edward Young's
Conjectures on Original Composition. (Modern Language Texts:
English Series; General Editor, W. P. Ker. Manchester: At the Uni-
versity Press; London and New York: Longmans, Green & Co., 1918.)
19·5 cm. pp. xviii + 64. Brief mention by James W. Bright in
Modern Language Notes, January 1920, XXXV, 58–62.

4. NINETEENTH CENTURY

(a) GENERAL

144. ASQUITH, HERBERT HENRY. Some Aspects of the Victorian Age. Oxford: The Clarendon Press. 1918. 23·5 cm. pp. 28. The Romanes Lecture, 1918. Brief mention by J. W. T[upper] in Modern Language Notes, January 1920, XXXV, 63–64.

145. BLORE, G. H. Victorian Worthies. Sixteen Biographies. 7¼ × 5¼. viii + 376 pp. London: H. Milford. 7s. 6d.

146. BRIE, FR. Aesthetische Weltanschauung in der Literatur des XIX. Jahrhunderts. Freiburg. 1921. pp. 80.

146 a. —— Exotismus der Sinne. Eine Studie zur Psychologie der Romantik. Heidelberg. 1920. pp. 79. Sitzungsberichte der Heidelberger Akademie der Wissenschaften, Philosoph.-Histor. Klasse, 1920.

147. CHUDOBA, FRANTIŠEK. Básníci, věštci a Bojovníci. Nová Řada. Poets, Prophets, and Fighters. New Series. 255 pp. Plzěn. Benísko. Price: 16 kč. Contents: Robert Browning. The Praeraphaelites. Ruskin's Praeterita. The Poetical Legacy of D. G. Rossetti. From the letters of George Meredith. Meredith's Poems.

147 a. —— Z Novější Literatury Swinburnovské. I. From recent literature on Swinburne. Zrání, vol. II, 1920. 49 n.

148. CLUTTON-BROCK, A. Essays on Books. (Including Dickens, Swinburne, Keats, etc.) 7 × 4¼. pp. 181. London: Methuen. 6s.

149. COLVIN, Sir SIDNEY. Some Personal Recollections. In Scribner's Mag., Jan.-March 1920, LXVII, 69–82, 210–23, 338–54. On Ruskin, Burne-Jones, Rossetti, Browning, Gladstone, Charles T. Newton, Trelawney, Victor Hugo, Gambetta, Stevenson.

150. COURTNEY, Mrs JANET ELIZABETH HOGARTH. Freethinkers of the Nineteenth Century. New York: E. P. Dutton & Co. 1920. 22·5 cm. pp. [x], 260. Front., ports. On Maurice, M. Arnold, Bradlaugh, Huxley, Leslie Stephen, Harriet Martineau, Kingsley. Reviewed in The Weekly Review, October 13, 1920, III, 322; in The New Republic, Aug. 11, 1920, XXIII, 313–4.

151. HANSTEIN, MARG. Die französische Literatur im Urteil der englischen Romantiker Wordsworth, Coleridge, Southey. Halle Diss. 1920. 127 pp. 8°.

152. HARPER, GEORGE McLEAN. John Morley and other Essays. Princeton, N.J.: Princeton University Press. 1920. 21 cm. pp. viii + 162. Contents: John Morley, Michelangelo's Sonnets, The Fame of Victor Hugo, Balzac's Human Comedy, An American Critic —W. C. Brownell, Wordsworth at Blois, Wordsworth's Love Poetry, David Brainard, a Puritan Saint.

153. HERZFELD, G. Aug. W. Schlegel in seinen Beziehungen zu englischen Dichtern und Kritikern. Archiv f. d. St. d. n. Spr. u. Lit. 139, 149–162.

30 BIBLIOGRAPHY

154. LANZA, Marquise CLARA. Literary New York in the 'Eighties. In The Bookman, March 1920, LI, 11–21.

155. PHILLIPS, WALTER C. Dickens, Reade, and Collins—Sensation Novelists. New York: Columbia Univ. Press. 1919. 21 cm. pp. ix, [3], 230. Columbia Univ. Studies in English and Comp. Lit. Rev. in The Nation, Jan. 10, 1920, CX, 47–8.

156. PIERCE, FREDERICK ERASTUS. Currents and Eddies in the English Romantic Generation. New Haven: Yale University Press. 1918. 23 cm. pp. 342. Reviewed by Robert Calvin Whitford in The So. Atlantic Quarterly, Jan. 1920, XIX, 84–5.

157. RUSSELL, Mrs FRANCES. Theresa Peet. Satire in the Victorian Novel. New York: Macmillan. 1920. 20·5 × 14 cm. pp. xiii, [2], 335. Bibl. note, pp. 317–27. Rev. in The Nation, July 10, 1920, CXI, 50.

158. THAYER, WILLIAM ROSCOE. Biography in the Nineteenth Century. In The No. Amer. Rev., May, June 1920, CCXI, 632–40, 826–33.

159. VILLARD, LÉONIE. La femme anglaise au dix-neuvième siècle, et son évolution d'après le roman anglais contemporain. 324 pp. 12 × 18. Didier, Paris. 5 f.

(b) AUTHORS

Arnold, Matthew. 160. FURRER, PAUL. Der Einfluss Sainte-Beuves auf die Kritik Matthew Arnolds. Zürcher Dissertation. 1920.

Arnold, Thomas. 161. Ensayos pedagógicos. Traducidos por L. Luzuriaga. Madrid: Tipográfica Renovación, 1920. 8°. 84 págs. Colección Universal (Calpe). o.30 ptas.

Austen, Jane. 162. AUSTEN-LEIGH, MARY AUGUSTA. Personal Aspects of Jane Austen. viii + 171 pp. London: Murray. 9s.

163. FIRKINS, OSCAR W. Jane Austen. New York: Henry Holt & Co. 1920. 19·5 cm. pp. ix + 254. Rev. by Horner E. Woodbridge in The Nation, Apr. 10, 1920, CX, 485.

Beaconsfield, Benj. Disraeli, Earl of. 164. Current Opinion. Disraeli Portrayed as the Eternal Romantic. Oct. 1920, LXIX, 521–4.

165. ABBOTT, WILBUR CORTEZ. An Accidental Victorian. In The Yale Rev., Apr. 1920, IX, 600–19.

166. GEYL, P. Disraeli. In De Gids, Sept. and Oct. 1920.

Beecher-Stowe, Harriet. 167. SCHNEIDER, ARTUR. Čiča Tomina Koliba pripovijetka iz života Crnaca u Sjevernoj Americi prije ukinuča robijaštva. Preveo sa slikama Sjube Babiča Mirko Breyer, Zagreb, 1920. Cijena 36 kruna—povezano.

Borrow, George. 168. Borrow, Jorge. La Biblia en España. Traducción directa del inglés por M. Azaña. Madrid. 8°. 2 vols. 351 y 305 págs. (Falta el 3° tomo.) Colección Granada. 2.50 ptas cada vol.

Brontë, Anne. 169. Complete Poems. Edited by Clement Shorter and C. W. Hatfield. Hodder and Stoughton. 12s. 6d.

Brontë, Charlotte. 170. DOOLEY, LUCILE. Psychoanalysis of Charlotte Brontë, as a Type of the Woman of Genius. Bibliog. In The Amer. Jour. of Psychology, July 1920, XXXI, 221–72.

171. KAVANAGH, COLMAN. The Symbolism of ' Wuthering Heights.' 7¼ × 4¾. pp. 30. John Long. 9d.

Browning, Elizabeth Barrett. 172. JOYCE, HEWETTE ELWELL. Mrs Browning's Contributions to American Periodicals. Modern Language Notes, XXXV, 7, November 1920, pp. 402–405.

Browning, Robert. 173. CLARKE, GEORGE HERBERT. Browning's A Blot in the 'Scutcheon: a Defence. In The Sewanee Review, Apr.-June 1920, XXVIII, 213–27.

174. COOK, A. K. A Commentary upon Browning's The Ring and the Book. Cr. 8vo. 7½ × 5. xxiii + 343 pp. Oxford Univ. Press. Rev. Time; Lit. Suppl., Sept. 23, 1920. 16s.

175. KAYE, FREDERICK BENJAMIN. Addison's Tye-Wig Preachment. Modern Language Notes, XXXV, 6, June 1920, p. 379.

176. LEWIS, EDWIN. The Making of The Ring and the Book. In The Methodist Review, March-April 1920, CIII, 237–52.

177. MAKON, ESTHER. A Triad of Symbols: the Bird, the Star and the Circle as used by Robert Browning. In Poet Lore, June 1920, XXXI, 284–90.

178. SALAZAR, F. Z. Il centenario della nascita di R. Browning. (Nuova Antologia, May 16.)

179. TANNER, ALEPT. Homage to Robert Browning. Waco, Texas. The Baylor Bulletin, Jan. 1920, XXIII, 1. 22·7 × 15·3 cm. pp. 151.

Butler, Samuel. 180. JONES, HENRY FESTING. Samuel Butler, Author of Erewhon (1835–1902): a Memoir. London: Macmillan. 1919. 21·9 × 14·5 cm. 2 vols. Reviewed by Maurice F. Egan in The New York Times Book Review, Jan. 15, 1920, pp. 1, 3; by Stuart P. Sherman in The Evening Post Book Review, Jan. 31, 1920, pp. 1, 4; by Clark S. Northup in Jour. Eng. and Germ. Philol., July 1920, XIX, 1; by Edmund Gosse in Edinburgh Rev., Jan. 1920.

181. LARBAUD, VALÉRY. Samuel Butler (étude et fragments traduits d'Erewhon). Nouv. Rev. Franç. Janv. 1920.

Byron. 182. ROE, HERBERT C. The Rare Quarto Edition of Lord Byron's 'Fugitive Pieces.' Described by. With a note on the Pigot family. Privately printed.

183. Selections from the Poems of Lord Byron. Cambridge: University Press (English Romantic Poets Series). xliv + 178 pp. 4s. 6d.

184. BADER, FR. Byroniana III. Der Verfasser des Uriel. Arch. f. d. St. d. n. Spr. u. Lit. 139, 214–217.

185. DALGADO, D. G. Lord Byron's Childe Harold's Pilgrimage to Portugal critically examined by.... Lisboa, 1919. 99 pags. Ed. da

Academia das Sciencias. 20·5 × 14·5 cm. (Só foi distribuido em 1920.)

186. FERRIMAN, Y. D. Lord Byron. Anglo-Hellenic League. 279 pp. 3*d*.

187. LOPES, DAVID. Parecer favoravel á publicação por conta da Academia do trabalho do sr. Dr. Dalgado intitulado 'Lord Byron's Childe Harold's Pilgrimage to Portugal.' V. Boletim da Segunda Classe da Academia das Sciencias. vol. 12°. pags. 368–370, 23. Coimbra, 1920.

188. LOCKWOOD, FRANK C. Byron, the Revolutionist. In The Methodist Review, March-Apr. 1920, CIII, 220–30.

189. ZACCHETTI, C. Lord Byron e l' Italia (Biblioteca di Scienza e Lettere, 71). Palermo: R. Sandron. 124 pp. 4.50 lire.

Carlyle. 190. FORNELLI, G. La Concezione storica di Tommaso Carlyle. Rivista di Cultura, Sept. 15.

191. POPOVIĆ. Francuska revolucija, La Bastille, I dio. Ćelap i, Zagreb, 1920 godine. Cijena 6.25 dinara.

191 *a*. —— Francuska revolucija, La Bastille, II dio. Ćelap i Popović, Zagreb, 1920 godine. Cijena 6.25 dinara.

192. Francuska Revolucija. S engleskog preveo i komentarom propratio Dr. Nikola Karlić. I deo: La Bastille. Druga sveska. Zagreb, 1919. 8-ina, 298 str. K. 15.

192 *a*. —— Francuska Revolucija. S engleskog preveo i komentarom propratio Dr. Nikola Karlić. I deo: La Bastille. Izdanje Jugoslov. Akad. Znanosti i Umetnosti. Cena K. 5.

193. RALLI, AUGUSTUS. Guide to Carlyle. 2 vols. 413, 456 pp. London: Allen and Unwin. 42*s*.

194. WILLIAMS, STANLEY T. Carlyle's Life of John Sterling. In The So. Atlantic Quarterly, Oct. 1920, XIX, 341–9.

Clemens, Samuel Langhorne (Mark Twain). 195. BRADFORD, GAMALIEL. Mark Twain. In The Atlantic Monthly, April 1920, CXXV, 462–73.

196. BROOKS, VAN WYCK. The Ordeal of Mark Twain. New York: E. P. Dutton & Co. Reviewed in The Weekly Review, Aug. 4, 1920, III, 108–9.

196 *a*. —— Mark Twain's Humour. In The Dial, March 1920, LXVIII, 275–91. Mark Twain's Satire. In The Dial, Apr. 1920, LXVIII, 424–43.

197. FARRÁN I MAYORAL, J. Critical Study of Mark Twain in 'Lletres a una amiga estrangera' (p. 84). Barcelona, 1920. Rev. by La Revista.

198. JOHNSON, ALVIN. The Tragedy of Mark Twain. In The New Republic, July 14, 1920, XXIII, 201–4.

199. MATTHEWS, BRANDER. Mark Twain and the Art of Writing. In Harper's, Oct. 1920, CXLI, 635–43.

200. PAINE, ALBERT BIGELOW. Letters of Mark Twain, with a Biographical Sketch and a Commentary. 9 × 6¼. xv + 433 pp.

Chatto and Windus. Rev. Times Lit. Suppl., 23 Sept. 1920, p. 615. 18s.

201. PECKHAM, H. HOUSTON. The Literary Status of Mark Twain, 1877–1890. In The South Atlantic Quarterly, Oct. 1920, XIX, 332–40.

Clough, Arthur Hugh. 202. OSBORNE, JAMES INSLEY. Arthur Hugh Clough. Boston: Houghton, Mifflin Company. 1920. 22½ × 14½ cm. Dissertation for Columbia University.

202a. —— Arthur Hugh Clough. Constable. 8vo. 9 × 5¾ pp. 195. Rev. Times Lit. Suppl., March 4, 1920. 8s. 6d.

Coleridge, Samuel Taylor. 203. GINGERICH, SOLOMON F. From Necessity to Transcendentalism in Coleridge. Publications of the Modern Language Association of America, XXXV, 1–59, March 1920.

204. RICHTER, HELENE. Die philosophische Weltanschauung von S. T. Coleridge und ihr Verhältnis zur deutschen Philosophie. Anglia, 44, 261–291, 297–325.

205. SAMPSON, GEORGE. Coleridge: Biographia Literaria. Chapters I–IV, XIV–XXII. Wordsworth: Prefaces and Essays on Poetry, 1800–1815. With an Introductory Essay by Sir Arthur Quiller-Couch. 8vo. 8 × 5½. pp. 367. C.U.P. 10s. net.

Dickens, Charles. 206. The Posthumous Papers of the Pickwick Club. Nelson. viii + 845 pp. 7s. 6d.

207. COR, RAPHAEL. Charles Dickens. Mer. de Fr. Vol. 141, pp. 82–99. 1920.

208. CROTCH, W. WALTER. The Touchstone of Dickens. Chapman and Hall. 8vo. 8¼ × 5½. pp. 197. 6s. net.

209. DIBBLE, ROY F. Charles Dickens: His Reading. Modern Language Notes, XXXV, 6, June 1920, pp. 334–339.

210. FIEDLER, FRITZ. Dickens und die Posse. Engl. St. 53, 370–405.

210a. —— Dickens' Belesenheit. Archiv für d. Stud. d. n. Spr. 140, 43–72.

210b. —— Dickens Gebrauch der rhythmischen Prosa im 'Christmas Carol.' Archiv f. d. St. d. n. Spr. u. Lit. 139, 47–50.

211. LEY, JAMES WILLIAM THOMAS. The Dickens Circle. New York: E. P. Dutton and Company. 1919. 22 cm. pp. xix, [2], 424. Front., plates, ports. Reviewed by Newman I. White in The So. Atlantic Quarterly, Jan. 1920, XIX, 82–4; by Leslie N. Broughton in The New Republic, Apr. 7, 1920, XXII, 191–2.

212. PHILLIPS, WALTER C. Dickens, Reade and Collins, Sensation Novelists. New York: Columbia University Press. London: Milford. xi + 230 pp. 8s. 6d.

213. POE, EDGAR ALLAN. English Notes: a Rare and Unknown Work; Being a Reply to Charles Dickens's American Notes; with Critical Comments by Joseph Jackson and George H. Sargent. New York: Lewis M. Thompson. 1920. 8vo. pp. 182. Originally pub. in Boston in 1842.

Eliot, George. 214. CHAFFURIN, LOUIS. Les amours de George Eliot. (3 art.) Grande Revue, Juillet-Sept. 1920.

215. CROSS, WILBUR LUCIUS. George Eliot in Retrospect. In The Yale Rev., Jan. 1920, IX, 256–70.

216. VINCENT, LEON H. A Note on George Eliot. In The Methodist Rev., Sept.-Oct. 1920, CIII, 712–22.

Emerson, Ralph Waldo. 217. Diario intimo. Traducción de L. de Terán, 1829–1839. Tomo I. 4°. 234 págs. 3 ptas.

218. Emerson's Essays; Selected and Edited by Arthur Hobson Quinn. New York: Scribner. 1920. 8vo. pp. xxiii + 298. The Modern Student's Library.

219. Veliki ljudi i napredak covjecanstva. Cena K. 1.

220. Historia y politica. Versión castellana por S. Valenti Camp. Barcelona: Dalman. 8°. 220 págs. 4 ptas.

221. Carlyle y Emerson. Epistolario. Traducción de L. de Terán. 4°. 311 págs. 6 ptas.

222. HUDSON, JAY WILLIAM. The Religion of Emerson. In The Sewanee Review, Apr.-June 1920, XXVIII, 203–12.

Gaskell, Mrs. 223. Mi prima Filis. Novela. La traducción del inglés ha sido hecha por P. Martinez Strong. Madrid: Tipográfica Renovación. 1920. 8°. 175 págs. 1 pta. (Colección Universal, Calpe.)

Harrison, Frederic. 224. HARRIS, MURIEL. Two Victorian Portraits. In The No. Amer. Rev., Sept. 1920, CCXII, 404–11. On Lord Morley and Frederic Harrison.

Hawthorne, Nathaniel. 225. Cuando la tierra era niña. Traducción de G. Martinez Sierra. Ilustraciónes de Fontanals. Madrid: Tipografia Artistica. 1920. 4°. 257 págs. 5 ptas. (Biblioteca Estrella.)

226. VAN DOREN, CARL. The Flower of Puritanism. In The Nation, Dec. 8, 1920, CXI, 649–50. On The Scarlet Letter.

227. HANSON, F. B. Nemesis in Hawthorne's Scarlet Letter. In The Methodist Review, Jan.-Feb. 1920, CIII, 71–82.

228. MATHERLY, ENID PUTNAM. Poe and Hawthorne as Writers of the Short Story. In Education, Jan. 1920, XL, 294–306.

Henley, William Ernest. 229. NEFF, MARIETTA. The Place of Henley. In The No. Amer. Rev., Apr. 1920, CCXI, 555–63.

Irving, Washington. 230. El legado del moro. Leyenda de la Alhambra. Versión castellana de N. Cossio de Jiménez. Madrid: Jiménez Fraud. 8°. 44 págs. 3.50 ptas.

James, Henry. 231. The Letters of Henry James. Selected and edited by Percy Lubbock. New York: Charles Scribner's Sons. 1920. Reviewed by Stuart P. Sherman in The Weekly Review, July 7, 1920, III, 706–7; by Stanley Went in The Unpartizan Review, July-Dec. 1920, XIV, 381–5; by Laurence Gilman in The No. Amer. Rev., May 1920, CCXI, 682–90; Times Lit. Suppl., April 8, 1920.

232. GOSSE, EDMUND. Henry James. In Scribner's Mag., Apr.-May 1920, LXVII, 422–30, 548–57.

ENGLISH LANGUAGE AND LITERATURE 35

233. LILJEGREN, S. B. American and European in the works of Henry James. pp. 58. Lunds Universitets Årsskrift. N.F. Avd. 1. Vol. 15–6. 3 kronor.

234. MATTHEWS, BRANDER. Henry James and the Theater. In The Bookman, June 1920, LI, 389–95.

235. NADAL, EHRMAN SYME. Personal Recollections of Henry James. In Scribner's Mag., July 1920, LXVIII, 89–97.

236. WHITFORD, ROBERT CALVIN. In The So. Atlantic Quarterly, Oct. 1920, XIX, 371–2.

Jerome, Jerome K. 237. FERRANDO, M. Jerome K. Jerome: Tres anglesos S'esbargeixen. Barcelona: Editorial Catalana. 8vo. pp. 196. (Biblioteca literária.) Rev. La Revista, 1920, p. 294.

Keats, John. 238. FEHR, BERNHARD. John Keats im Lichte der neuesten Forschung. Archiv für das Studium der neueren Sprachen und Literaturen, 139 (1920), 163–178. Braunschveig: George Westermann. 1920.

238a. —— Keats dichterische Glosse zu Francis Bacon. Engl. Stud. 54, 326–8

239. MANENT, MARIA. John Keats: Sonets i Odes. Preface by Eugeni d'Ors. La Revista series of 'World Lyrics.' Barcelona. 1919.

240. NOTCUTT, H. CLEMENT. An Interpretation of Keats's Endymion. By H. Clement Notcutt, Professor of English in the University of Stellenbosch, South Africa. (Printed for the Author by the South African Electric Printing Co., Capetown, 1919.) Reviewed by J. W. B[right] in Modern Language Notes, May 1920, XXXV, 316–320.

Kingsley, Charles. 241. WILLIAMS, STANLEY T. Yeast: a Victorian Heresy. In The No. Amer. Rev., Nov. 1920, CCXII, 697–704.

Lamb, Charles. 242. LUCAS, E. V. Essays of Elia. (Introduction and notes by.) Methuen, 5s.

243. WOODS, GEORGE B. A Note on Lamb. Modern Language Notes, XXXV, 5, May 1920, p. 315. Note.—Locates a phrase used by Lamb.

Landor, Walter Savage. 244. Lirica inglesa: Epitafio. Trad. de Pedro Guirao. Estudio, 1920, XXXI, 70.

Locker-Lampson, Frederick. 245. BIRRELL, AUGUSTINE. Frederick Locker-Lampson. A Character Sketch. Constable. ix + 206 pp. Rev. Times Lit. Suppl., June 17, 1920. 25s.

Longfellow, Henry Wadsworth. 246. BOGGESS, ARTHUR C. The Old Testament in Longfellow's Poems. In The Methodist Review, March-April 1920, CIII, 263–71.

247. DUNN, ESTHER CLOUDMAN. Longfellow the Teacher. In The No. Amer. Rev., Feb. 1920, CCXI, 259–65.

248. FERRA, MIQUEL. Les muses Amigues. H. W. Longfellow translated into Catalan Verse. p. 43. Sóller. 1920.

249. REA, JOHN DOUGAN. Longfellow's Nature. In Modern Philology, May 1920, XVIII, 48.

BIBLIOGRAPHY

Lowell, Amy. 250. WILKINSON, Mrs MARGUERITE OGDEN BIGE-LOW (HARLEY GRAVES, pseud.). Amy Lowell. In The Touchstone, June 1920, VII, 219–20.

Lowell, James Russell. 251. JOYCE, HEWETTE ELWELL. A Bibliographical Note on James Russell Lowell. Modern Language Notes, XXXV, 4, April 1920, pp. 249–250.

—— 252. SMITH, FREDERICK D. Mr Wilbur's Postumous Macaronics. In Quart. Jour. Univ. No. Dakota, July 1920, X, 436–43. A study of the Biglow Papers, 2nd ser. 8.

253. THAYER, WILLIAM ROSCOE. James Russell Lowell as a Teacher: Recollections of His Last Pupil. In Scribner's Mag., Oct. 1920, LXVIII, 473–80.

254. The Function of the Poet, and other Essays. Collected and edited by Albert Mordell. Boston: Houghton, Mifflin Company. 1920. 21 cm. pp. [2], xi, [1], 223, [1]. 575 copies. Reviewed by Laurence Gilman in The No. Amer. Rev., Aug. 1920, CCXII, 267–72; in The Nation, Aug. 14, 1920, CXI, 191.

255. TOWNSEND, FRANK S. James Russell Lowell. In The Methodist Rev., Sept.-Oct. 1920, CIII, 763–9.

Macaulay, Thomas Babington, Lord. 256. DEARBORN, A. R. Macaulay Up to Date. In The Sewanee Review, Jan.-March 1920, XXVIII, 66–74.

257. Essay on Clive. Edited with introduction and notes by E. H. Elliott. pp. 210. Publishers: Śrīnivāsa Varadācan & Co., Madras. 8°. 1st ed. Price Rs. 1.4.

258. History of England, chapters 1–3. Edited by W. F. Reddaway. pp. 425. Publishers: Macmillan & Co., Ltd, Bombay. 8°. 1st edition. Price Rs. 3.

259. Lives of Bunyan and Goldsmith. Edited with introduction and notes, etc., by A. M. S. Rāghavan. pp. 267. Published by C. Subbayya Ceṭṭi & Co., Madras. (Dec. 1919.) 8°. 2nd edition, revised. Price Rs. 1.8.

260. Lord Clive. Edited with introduction, and notes by R. S. Sheppard. pp. 300. Published by P. R. Rama Ayyar & Co., Madras. (Aug. 1920.) 8°. 1st edition. Price 12 annas.

261. Essay on Addison. With an elaborate introduction, full explanatory and critical notes, etc. pp. 360. Published by C. Subbayya Ceṭṭi & Co., Madras. (June 1920.) 8°. 1st edition. Price Rs. 1.8.

Meredith, George. 262. ELLIS, S. M. George Meredith. His Life and Friends in relation to his Work. 8vo. 9 × 5¾. pp. 326. Grant Richards. 21s.

263. TORRETTA, L. George Meredith romanziere, poeta, pensatore. pp. 239. Napoli, Perrella.

Mitford. 264. HILL, CONSTANCE. Mary Russell Mitford and her surroundings. 8vo. 9 × 5¾. xiv + 387. John Lane. 21s.

Moore, Thomas. 265. TALLADA, J. M. L'Utopia de Tomás More. Barcelona: La Revista. p. 83. 1920.

Morley, John, Viscount. 266. HARRIS, MURIEL. Two Victorian Portraits. In The No. Amer. Rev., Sept. 1920, CCXII, 404-11. On Lord Morley and Frederic Harrison.

Morris, William. 267. MACKAIL, J. W. Life of William Morris. 2 volumes. I, 375 pp. II, 364 pp. Longmans. 28s.

268. PENNELL, ELIZABETH ROBINS. Some memories of William Morris. In Amer. Mag. of Art, Feb. 1920, XI, 124-7.

269. TALLADA, J. M. Les Utopies Comunistes: Noves d'enhloc, by William Morris. Barcelona: La Revista. 1920. ptas. 50.

270. VIDALENC, G. William Morris. 168 pp. 15 × 20·5. Alcan, Paris. 5 f.

Pater, Walter. 271. KIRK, RICHARD R. A Sentence by Walter Pater. In Jour. Eng. and Germ. Philol., July 1920, XIX, 365-76.

272. SHAFER, ROBERT. Walter Pater Redivivus. In The Open Court, April 1920. XXXIV, 217-31.

Patmore, Coventry. 273. SYMONS, ARTHUR. Coventry Patmore. In The No. Amer. Rev., Feb. 1920, CCXI, 266-72.

Poe, Edgar Allan. 274. Anon. trad. Le système du Docteur Goudron. 64 pp. A. Michel, Paris. 2 f.

275. CAMPBELL, K. The Poe-Griswold Controversy. Pub. Mod. Lang. Ass. Am. 24.3.

276. Cuentos clásicos del Norte. Primera serie por Edgar Allan Poe. Segunda serie por Washington Irving, Nathániel Hawthorne, Edward Everett Hale. Traducción de C. Torres Calderón de Pinillos. New York: Doubleday, Sage and Company. 1920. (Biblioteca Interamericana.)

277. FARRÁN I MAYORAL, J. Critical study of Edgar Allan Poe in 'Lletres a una amiga estrangera.' p. 170. Barcelona. 1920. Ed. by La Revista.

278. MABBOTT, THOMAS OLLIVE. A Few Notes on Poe. Modern Language Notes, XXXV, 6, June 1920, pp. 372-374.

279. MATHERLY, ENID PUTNAM. Poe and Hawthorne as Writers of the Short Story. In Education, Jan. 1920, XL, 294-306.

280. SMITH, CHARLES ALPHONSO. Poe and the Bible. In The Biblical Review, July 1920, V, 354-65.

281. Poe, Edgar Allan, English Notes: A rare and unknown work. *See under* Dickens, Charles.

282. YEWDALE, MERTON S. Edgar Allan Poe, Pathologically. In The No. Amer. Rev., Nov. 1920, CCXII, 686-96.

283. Leve discusión con una momia. Traducción de M. Abril. 16°. 76 págs. 1.50 ptas.

284. Historias extraordinarias: Metzengerstein, El misterio de María Roget, El demonio de la perversidad, El gato negro, Guillermo Wilson, El hambre de las muchedumbres, El corazón revelador, Bernice. Traducida de la de C. Baudelaire por E. Ramírez Angel. 8°. 221 págs. 3 ptas.

285. Nuevas historias extraordinarias: Conversación de Eiros con

38 BIBLIOGRAPHY

Charmión, Sombra, Silencio, La isla del Hada, El retrato ovalado, El jugador de ajedrez de Madzel, Eleonoro, Un acontecimiento en Jerusalén, El ángel de lo grotesco, El sistema del doctor 'Alquitrán' y del profesor 'Plumá,' El dominio de Ariheim, La finca de Landor. Traducción de A. González Blanco. 8º. 218 págs. 3 ptas.

286. Nuevas historias extraordinarias. VI: Eureka o ensayo sobre el universo material y espiritual. Traducción de R. Cansinos-Assens. Madrid: Mateu. 8º. 209 págs. 2.50 ptas.

287. Historias extraordinarias: Singular aventura de Hans Pfaall, Manuscrito encontrado en una botella, Un descenso al Maelstrom, El verdadero caso del Sr Valdemar, Revelación magnética, Los recuerdos de Augusto Bedloe-Morella, Ligeia. Traducción de J. Francés. 8º. 201 págs. 3 ptas.

288. Nuevas historias extraordinarias. Traducción de R. Gómez de la Serna. 8º. 227 págs. 3 ptas.

289. Cuentos de lo grotesco y lo arabesco. Traducción y prólogo de R. Lasso de la Vega. 8º. 280 págs. 4 ptas.

Riley, James Whitcomb. 290. BEERS, HENRY AUGUSTUS. The Singer of the Old Swimmin' Hole. In The Yale Rev., Jan. 1920, IX, 395–402.

Robinson, Edward Arlington. 291. MACKAYE, PERCY. E. A.—a Milestone for America. In The No. Amer. Rev., Feb. 1920, CCXI, 121–7.

Rossetti, Dante Gabriel. 292. TROMBLY, ALBERT EDMUND. Rossetti Studies. In The So. Atlantic Quarterly, July 1919, Jan. 1920, XVIII, 211–21, 341–9; XIX, 67–80.

Ruskin, John. 293. GRAHAM, JOHN W. The Harvest of Ruskin. Cr. 8vo. 7½ × 5. pp. 270. G. Allen and Unwin. 7s. 6d. net.

294. Ruskin the Prophet, and other Centenary Studies. By John Masefield, Dean Inge, C. F. G. Masterman and others. Edited by J. Howard Whitehouse. 8vo. 8¼ × 5½. pp. 157. G. Allen and Unwin. 8s. 6d.

Scott, Sir Walter. 295. MAIGRON, L. Walter Scott. Paris: Renaiss. du Livre. 4 fr.

296. WITHINGTON, ROBERT. Scott's Contribution to Pageantic Development—a Note on the Visit of George IV to Edinburgh in 1822. In Studies in Philology, April 1920, XVII, 121–5.

Shelley, Percy Bysshe. 297. A Philosophical View of Reform. Transcribed and prepared for press by T. W. Rolleston. Milford.

298. HUSCHER, H. Studien zu Shelley's Lyrik. Leipziger Beitr. f. engl. Philol. Her. v. Max Förster. 1. Heft. 1919. 156 pp. Gr. 8º. Leipzig: B. Tauchnitz. 10 Mk.

299. MADARIAGA, SALVADOR DE. Shelley and Calderon, and other Essays on English and Spanish Poetry. London: Constable. 1920. 15s.

300. RAYMONDI, R. P. B. Shelley in Italia. Padova: Zannoni.

301. PANCOAST, HENRY SPACKMAN. Shelley's Ode to the West

Wind. Modern Language Notes, XXXV, 2, February 1920, pp. 97–100.

Spencer, Herbert. 302. SARTON, GEORGE. Herbert Spencer, 1820–1920. In Scribner's Mag., June 1920, LXVII, 695–703.

Stevenson. 303. Anon. trad. Le Maître de Ballantrae. 330 pp. In 8°. La Sirène, Paris. 7 f. 50.

304. BAY, JENS CHRISTIAN. Echoes of Robert Louis Stevenson. Chicago: W. M. Hill. 1920. 8vo. pp. 93. Portr., facsims.

305. BROWN, GEORGE E. The Book of R. L. S.; Works, Travels, Friends, and Commentators. New York: Scribner. 1920. Rev. in The Nation, Apr. 3, 1920, CX, 436.

306. CECCHI, EMILIO. Il vero Stevenson [in] La Tribuna (Rome), 20 August 1920. [The true Stevenson Cecchi finds above all in the letters and diaries, and in the pages of In the South Seas, in which he perceives 'una familiare chiarezza anche superiore a quella sua chiarezza temperata su Livio; una naturale finitezza, anche più raffinata di quella sua industriosa finitezza quasi francese.']

307. GUTHRIE, LORD. Robert Louis Stevenson, some personal recollections. Edinburgh: W. Green and Sons. 21s.

308. KINGSLEY, MAUDE ELMA. Outline Study of David Balfour. In Education, Dec. 1920, XLI, 226–41.

309. SAVINE, A. et GEORGES-MICHEL trad. Les hommes joyeux. 256 pp. 12 × 19. Edit. fr. ill. Paris. 5 f. 50.

310. WATT, LAUCHLAN MACLEAN. Robert Louis Stevenson's Contribution to Literature and Life. In Scribner's Mag., Dec. 1920, LXVIII, 641–53.

311. El extraño caso del Dr Jekyll y Mr Hide. Novela. Traducción de J. Torroba. Madrid: Tipográfica Renovación. 1920. Colección Universal (Calpe).

Swinburne, Algernon Charles. 312. CHEW, SAMUEL C. Swinburne's Contributions to The Spectator in 1862. Modern Language Notes, XXXV, 2, February 1920, 118–119.

313. KERNAHAN, COULSON. Swinburne as I knew Him. London: John Lane. 1919. 19 cm. pp. xiii, [2], 108. Rev. in The Review, May 20, 1920, II, 576.

Symonds, John Addington. 314. Studies of the Greek Poets. A. and C. Black. 609 pp. 21s.

Tennyson, Alfred. 315. DIXON, JAMES MAIN. The Spiritual Meaning of In Memoriam. Boston. The Abingdon Press. 1920. Interpretation for the Times. Introduction by James M. Campbell. New York: The Abingdon Press. [1920.] 19·5 cm. pp. 173.

316. PYRE, JAMES FRANCIS AUGUSTIN. The Formation of Tennyson's Style. Madison, Wis.: The Univ. of Wisconsin. 1920. Univ. of Wisconsin Studies in Language and Literature 12.

317. SIDEY, THOMAS K. Some Unnoted Latinisms in Tennyson. Modern Language Notes, XXXV, 4, April 1920, pp. 245–246.

318. VAN DYKE, HENRY. Studies in Tennyson. New York:

Scribner. 1920. 20 cm. pp. xii, [3], 316. Front. (port.). A new edition. First published in 1889.

319. Poems of Tennyson, Chosen and Edited with an introduction by Henry Van Dyke. New York: Scribner. 1920. 8vo. pp. cxx + 342. First pub. in 1903. A new edition.

Thackeray, William Makepeace. 320. Catalina. Novela. Traducción de M. Alarcón. Madrid: Tipográfica Renovación. 1920. Colección Universal (Calpe).

321. ELY, CATHERINE BEACH. The Psychology of Becky Sharp. Modern Language Notes, XXXV, 1, January 1920, pp. 31–33.

322. VAN DYKE, HENRY. Writers We Love to Read. i. Thackeray and Real Men. In Harper's, Jan. 1920, CXL, 172–8.

323. VOGEL, GUDRUN. Thackeray als historischer Romanschriftsteller. Leipziger Beitr. f. engl. Phil. Her. v. M. Förster. 2. Heft. 1920. 105 pp. Gr. 8°. Leipzig: B. Tauchnitz. 8 Mk.

Thoreau, Henry David. 324. SHEPARD, ODELL. The Paradox of Thoreau. In Scribner's Mag., Sept. 1920, LXVIII, 335–42.

Trollope, Anthony. 325. RANDELL, W. L. Anthony Trollope and his Work. Fortn. Rev., Sept. 1920.

326. SAINTSBURY, GEORGE. Trollope Revisited. *See* Essays and Studies by The English Association. X. 392.

Whitman, Walt. 327. BAZALGETTE, LÉON. Walt Whitman, the Man and His Work. Translated by Ellen FitzGerald. Garden City, New York: Doubleday, Page & Co. 1920. 21 cm. pp. xviii + 355, [1]. The original was published in 1908. Rev. by John Black in The Bookman, April 1920, LI, 172–4.

328. —— Calamus. Poèmes. Version nouvelle. Avec 10 bois hors-texte dessinés et gravés par Frans Masereel. iv + 107 pp. In 8°. Genève (Editions du Sablier). 1919. 15 f.

329. BLACK, JOHN. Walt Whitman: Fiction-Writer and Poets' Friend. In The Bookman, April 1920, LI, 172–4.

330. CÉ, CAMILLE [pseudon. de Chemin]. Le poète-prophète Walt Whitman. Grande Revue. pp. 573–99. Févr. 1920.

331. HOLLOWAY, R. EMERY. Walt Whitman's Love Affairs. In The Dial, Nov. 1920, LXIX, 473–83.

332. LESSING, OTTO EDUARD. Horace Tranbel, Whitman's Friend and Biographer. In The Open Court, Jan., Feb. 1920, XXXIV, 49–62, 87–97, to be contin.

333. MONTOLIN, CEBRIÀ DE. Walt Whitman: 'Doneu me l'esplèndid sol silencios...' Catalan translation. Messidar. 1918–1920. p. 40.

334. SÉLINCOURT, ERNEST DE. Leaves of Grass by Walt Whitman. Selected and edited with an Introduction. (World's Classics.) Oxford: Univ. Press. 2s. 6d., 4s. 6d.

335. SHAY, FRANK. The Bibliography of Walt Whitman. New York: Friedman's. 1920.

Wilde, Oscar. 336. BAEZA, R. Un marido ideal. Comedia en cuatro actos. Traducción. Madrid. 8°. 168 págs. 2.50 ptas.

337. CASTRO, C. DE. El abanico de lady Windermere. Comedia. Traducción. Cartagena-Madrid: Artes Gráficas. 8°. 136 págs. 2 ptas.

338. FÉLIPE, LÉON. El renacimiento del Arte inglés y otros ensayos. Traducción. Madrid: Juan Pueyo. 1920. 8°. 237 págs. 3.50 ptas. (Editorial América.)

339. HARRIS, FRANK. Oscar Wilde: His Life and Confessions. 2 vols. 8vo. 8 × 5¼. pp. 327, 289. London: Frank Harris. 42s.

340. Priče. Zagreb, 1920. Tzdanje knjižare Mirka Breyera. 8°. Cena 10 dinara.

341. RICHTER, HELENE. Oscar Wilde's Persönlichkeit in seinen Gedichten. Engl. Stud. 54, 201–277.

342. SCHNEIDER, ARTUR. Dorian Gray. Sengleskoga preveo. St Kugli, Zagreb, 1920 god. 218 pp. 20 × 13·5. Cena 14 dinara.

343. SERNA, J. GOMEZ DE LA. Intenciones. Ensayos de literatura y estética. Traducción. Madrid. 1920. 8°. 3.50 ptas. (Biblioteca Nueva.)

343a. —— El retrato de Dorian Gray. Traducción. Madrid. 8°. 330 págs. 3.50 ptas.

344. SYMONS, ARTHUR. A Jester with Genius. In The Bookman, Apr. 1920, LI, 129–34.

345. THOMAS, LOUIS. L'esprit d'Oscar Wilde. 200 pp. 12 × 18·5. Crès, Paris. 6 f.

346. VELIKANOVIĆ, Iso. Mladi kralj i druge pripovijesti. Sengleskog preveo. Uresio Ljuba Babić. Mirko Breyer, Zagreb, 1920 god. Cijena 60 kruna.

347. ZLOČINSTVO, LORDA ARTURA SEVILA. Izdanje Ognjanovičeve Univerzalne Biblioteke, br. 12. N. Sad. 1920. 16-ina. 78 str. Din. 1.50.

Wordsworth, William. 348. BROUGHTON, LESLIE NATHAN. The Theocritean Element in the Works of William Wordsworth. vii + 193 pp. 23 × 14 cm. Halle: Max Niemeyer. M. 14 net. 1920.

349. CAMPBELL, OSCAR JAMES. Sentimental Morality in Wordsworth's Narrative Poetry. In Studies by Members of the Dept. of English. Madison, Wis. 1920. Univ. of Wisconsin Studies in Lang. and Lit. 11.

350. DUNN, ESTHER CLOUDMAN. Inman's Portrait of Wordsworth. In Scribner's Mag., Feb. 1920, LXVII, 251–6. Illus.

351. KNOWLTON, EDGAR COLBY. The Novelty of Wordsworth's Michael as a Pastoral. In Publ. Mod. Lang. Assn America, Dec. 1920, XXXV, 432–46.

352. POTTS, ABBIE FINDLAY. Wordsworth and the Bramble. In Jour. Eng. and Germ. Philol., July 1920, XIX, 340–49.

353. SAMPSON, GEORGE. See Coleridge.

5. TWENTIETH CENTURY

(a) GENERAL

354. ABTHORN, J. The Arts and Living. London: W. Heinemann. 6s.

355. ANTHORN, EDITH. Vom Englischen Soldatenlied. G.R.M. VIII, 29–45.

356. AUSTIN, MARY HUNTER. New York: Dictator of American Criticism. In The Nation, July 31, 1920, CXI, 129–30.

356a. —— Supernaturals in Fiction. In The Unpartizan Review, March-April 1920, XIII, 236–45.

357. BAKER, HARRY T. The Contemporary Short Story. A practical Manual. Roy. 8vo. 9½ × 5. pp. 280. Heath. 7s. 6d.

357a. —— Periodicals and Permanent Literature. In The No. Amer. Rev., Dec. 1920, CCXII, 777–87.

358. BAKER, RAY PALMER. A History of English-Canadian Literature to the Confederation: Its Relation to the Literature of Great Britain and the United States. Cambridge: Harvard Univ. Press. 1920. 20·6 × 14·5 cm. pp. xi, [1], 200.

359. BALDENSPERGER, F. Les tendances de la poésie aux Etats Unis au début de la guerre. [4 articles.] France—Etats Unis. Fev., Mars. Mai 1920 et Jan. 1921.

360. BAYLEY, JOHN. Poetry and the Commonplace (British Academy Warton Lectures on English Poetry, No. 10). Roy. 8vo. Oxford University Press. 1s. 6d.

361. BEERS, HENRY AUGUSTUS. Four Americans: Roosevelt, Hawthorne, Emerson, Whitman. Cr. 8vo. O.U.P. 4s. 6d.

361a. —— The Connecticut Wits and Other Essays. New Haven: Yale University Press. 1920. Reviewed in The Weekly Review, Nov. 24, 1920, III, 506.

362. BEZA, M. English Poets of To-day—Ideea Europeană. Anul, II, No. 50–51. In two numbers of this weekly Review M. Beza traces the new tendencies of the contemporary English poets dealing mostly with the following: John Masefield, William Davies, Walter de la Mare, James Elroy Flecker, Rupert Brooke.

363. BRAITHWAITE, WILLIAM STANLEY BEAUMONT. The Book of Modern British Verse. Boston: Small, Maynard Co. 1920. Rev. by Robert P. Utter in The Nation, Feb. 21, 1920, CX, 238.

364. British Academy, Proceedings of, 1917–1918. Milford.

365. BROOKE, STOPFORD A. Naturalism in English Poetry. London: Dent. 1920. 7s. 6d.

366. BRUNNER, KARL. Die Dialektliteratur von Lancashire Publikationen der Hochschule für Welthandel. 59 pp. 8°. Wien, Verlag der Hochschule für Welthandel. 10 Kronen.

367. BURROUGHS, JOHN. What Makes a Poem? In The Bookman, October 1920, LII, 102–7.

368. CAIRNS, WILLIAM B. British Criticisms of American Writings, 1783–1815: a Contribution to the Study of Anglo-American Literary Relationships. Madison, Wis. 1918. 23½ cm. pp. 98. University of Wisconsin Studies in Language and Literature 1. Reviewed by Killis Campbell in Jour. Eng. and Germanic Philol., Apr. 1920, XIX, 302–3.

369. CANBY, HENRY SEIDEL. Literature in a Democracy. In The Century, Jan. 1920, XCIX, 396–401.

370. CARDEN, PERCY T. The Murder of Edwin Drood—a new solution of the mystery. Cecil Palmer. xviii + 125 pp. 6s.

371. CARDIM, LUIZ. Torrent of Portyngale. V. Revista da Faculdade de Letros da Universidade do Porto, Nos. 1–2, pags. 116–136. 24 × 16·5 cm. Porto. 1920.

Catalan Translations. 372. ALDINGTON, RICHARD. Images of War. La Revista, 1920, p. 60. L'Alba. Ibid. p. 37. BALDERSTON, JOHN L. The Genius of Marne. Bibl. Notes in La Veu de Catalunya, July 4, 1920. CARNER, JOSEP. El Papat i els Temps moderns esbòs politic per William Barry. Enciclopedia Catalana. 8vo. pp. 178. 1919. BODENHEIM, MAXWELL. 'A un enemie' i 'El Minaire.' La Revista, 1920, p. 36. FROST, ROBERT. El meu hoste de Novembre. Ibid. 1920, p. 35. KREYMBERG, ALFRED. 'America' and 'Old Manuscript.' Ibid. p. 36. MASTERS, EDGAR LEE. Silenci. Ibid. p. 33. LOWELL, AMY. 'Chinoi series,' 'Reflexions,' 'Caient neu i Gebre.' Ibid. pp. 37–38. MASEFIELD, JOHN. 'Que sóc, vida?' 'Mirant.' Ibid. p. 38. MEYNELL, ALICE. Maternitat. Ibid. p. 38. MONRO, HAROLD. Un ciuitat gran.' POUND, EZRA. 'La vinguda de la guerra,' 'Acteu in Ortus.' Ibid. p. 35. SANDBURG, KARL. 'Perduda,' 'Killers i Chicago.' Ibid. pp. 34, 35. UPWARD, ALLEN. Fulles oloroses d'un gerro xinès. Ibid. pp. 39–40. LAWRENCE, D. H. Cuques de llum en el blat. Ibid. p. 37. ROBINSON, EDWIN ARLINGTON. Casandra. Ibid. p. 33. WILLIAMS, WILLIAM CARLES. 'Figura mètrica' i 'Moviment pausat.' Ibid. p. 36. *See also* FARRAN, J. 1 MAYORAL, Lletres a una amiga estrangera, for references to Bacon, Dickens, William James, Goldsmith, B. Shaw, etc.

373. CATEL, JEAN. La poésie américaine d'aujourd'hui. Mercure de Fr., vol. 138, pp. 601–27. Mars 1920.

374. CAZAMIAN, LOUIS. L'évolution psychologique et la littérature en Angleterre (1660–1914). 268 pp. 12 × 18·5. Alcan, Paris. 13 f.

375. CHESTERTON, G. K. The Uses of Diversity. A Book of Essays. Cr. 8vo. 7 × 4¼. pp. 197. Methuen. 6s.

376. CLARKE, GEORGE HERBERT, ed. A Treasury of War Poetry. Second Series. Boston: Houghton, Mifflin Co. 1919. 18 cm. pp. xxxvii + 361, [1]. Rev. by Robert P. Utter in the Nation, Feb. 21, 1920, CX, 237–8.

377. COLBY, ELTRIDGE. The Echo-Device in Literature. New York. The Public Library. 1920. 25·5 cm. pp. 61. Reprinted from

the Bulletin of the New York Public Library, Nov., Dec. 1919, XXIII, 683–713, 783–804.

378. COLLINS, JOSEPH. Idling in Italy: Studies of Literature and of Life. New York: Scribner. 1920. 21 cm. pp. x, [2], 316. Includes Fictional Biography and Autobiography; The Literary Mausoleum of Samuel Butler. Rev. in The No. Amer. Rev., Dec. 1920, CCXII, 856–9.

379. COOK, HOWARD WILLARD. Makers of Modern American Poetry. In The Mentor, June 15, 1920, VIII, i–ii.

380. COSTA, FERNANDES. O arcade curvo Semmedo na poesia anglo-americana. Influencias litterarias peninsulares em alguns poetas ingleses do começo do seculo XIX. V. Boletim da Segunda Classe da Academia das Sciencias, vol. 12°. pags. 587–607. 23·5 × 14·5 cm. Coimbra. 1920.

381. CUTLER, FRANCES WENTWORTH. Soldier-Poets of England. In The Sewanee Review, Jan.-March 1920, XXVIII, 85–92.

382. DARWIN, Sir FRANCIS. Springtime and other Essays. Cr. 8vo. 7½ × 5. pp. 253. Murray. 7s. 6d.

383. DAVIES, T. H. Spiritual Voices in Modern Literature. London: Hodder and Stoughton. 1920. 8s. 6d.

384. DAVIS, FRANKLIN PIERRE, ed. Anthology of Newspaper Verse for 1919. Enid, Okla.: P. F. Davis Co. 1920.

385. D'HANGEST, G. Orthodoxie et Autonomie [étude du roman de Cath. Carswell: Open the door]. Les Langues Modernes, pp. 513–32, Nov.-Déc. 1920.

386. EDMUNDS, E. W. An Historical Summary of English Literature. London: Carvell. 1920. 7½ × 5¼. viii + 276 pp. 5s.

387. ELIOT, T. S., HUXLEY, ALDOUS, FLINT, F. S. Three Critical Essays on Modern English Poetry. Chapbook No. 9. (The Poetry Book-shop.) Rev. Times Lit. Suppl., April 15, 1920. 1s. 6d.

388. ELIOT, T. S., The Sacred Wood (Essays on Poetry and Criticism). London: Methuen. 1920. 7 × 4½. xviii + 155 pp. 6s.

389. ELLIS, HAVELOCK. The Philosophy of Conflict and Other Essays in War-Time. Boston: Houghton, Mifflin Company. 1919. 20·5 cm. pp. 299. Includes essays on Herbert Spencer, Mr Conrad's World, Cowley.

390. ELTON, OLIVER. A Survey of English Literature, 1830–1880. London: Arnold. 1920. 8¾ × 5¾. Vol. I. xvi + 434 pp. Vol. II. xi + 432 pp. 32s.

391. Poems of To-day. An Anthology. Published for the English Association by Sidgwick and Jackson. 3s.

392. Essays and Studies by Members of the English Association. Vol. VI. Collected by A. C. BRADLEY. 8vo. 8¾ × 5¾. pp. 145. Oxford: Univ. Press. Contents: 1, The Caedmonian Genesis, by Henry Bradley; 2, The Humanist Ideal, by W. P. Ker; 3, Trollope Revisited, by George Saintsbury; 4, On Playing the Sedulous Ape, by George Sampson; 5, Conrad, by F. Melian Stawell; 6, South Eastern and South East Midland Dialects, by H. C. Wyld. 6s. 6d.

393. ERSKINE, JOHN (ed. by). 'Life and Literature': Lafcadio Hearn. London: Heinemann. 1920. 9¼ × 6¼. x + 393 pp. 25s.

394. ERVINE, ST JOHN GREER. Concerning Heroes. In The New Republic, June 9, 1920, XXIII, 47–9.

394a. —— Literary Taste in America. In The New Republic, October 6, 1920, XXIV, 144–7.

394b. —— Some Impressions of My Elders. In The No. Amer. Rev., Feb.-Aug. 1920, CCXI, 225–37, 402–10, 669–; CCXII, 118–28, 238–49. On W. B. Yeats, Bernard Shaw, J.M.Synge, H.G.Wells, A. E.

395. FIGUEIREDO, FIDELINO DE. Bibliographia das escriptas portugueses sobre as litteraturas inglesa e norte-americana e sobre as relações litterarias de Portugal com a Inglaterra a os Estados Unidos. V. A Critica Litteraria Como Sciencia, Lisboa, 1920. 22·5 × 14·5 cm. Edição da Livraria Classica Editora, P. dos Restauradores, 17, Lisboa. Esta materia esté comprehendida no capitulo da secção do appendice intitulado Bibliographia Portuguesa de Critica Litteraria.

396. FOLLETT, HELEN THOMAS and WILSON. Some Modern Novelists. 7¾ × 5¼. ix + 368 pp. Allen and Unwin. 7s. 6d.

397. FULLER, HENRY BLAKE. The American Image as It appears to Jean Catel. In Poetry, March 1920, XV, 327–31.

398. GAYLEY, CHARLES MILLS, and BENJAMIN PUTNAM KURTZ. Methods and Materials of Literary Criticism: Lyric, Epic, and Allied Forms of Poetry. Boston: Ginn & Co. 1920. 19×17·5cm. pp. xi+911.

399. GEROULD, KATHARINE FULLERTON. Modes and Morals. New York: Scribner. 1920. 19·5 cm. pp. [vi], 278. Includes Miss Alcott's New England; British Novelists, Ltd.; The Remarkable Rightness of Rudyard Kipling. Rev. by Dorothy Brewster in The Nation, Apr. 10, 1920, CX, 486–8.

400. GOOCH, G. P. Historical Novels. Cont. Review, Feb. 1920.

401. GRAHAM, WALTER. Poets of the American Ambulance. In The So. Atlantic Quarterly, Jan. 1920, XIX, 18–23.

402. HANEY, JOHN LOUIS. English Literature. New York: Harcourt, Brace and Howe. 1920. 8vo. pp. xii + 452. Rev. by Geo. H. Clarke in The Sewanee Rev., Oct.-Dec. 1920, XXVIII, 606–7.

403. HAVENS, GEORGE R. The Abbé Le Blanc and English Literature. In Modern Philology, Dec. 1920, XVIII, 423–41.

404. HELLER, OTTO. Convention and Revolt in Poetry. In Washington Univ. Studies, Apr. 1920, VII, 163–85. St Louis.

405. H[ENDERSON], A[LICE] C[ORTIN]. The Folk Poetry of these States. In Poetry, Aug. 1920, XVI, 264–73.

406. HENLEY, WILLIAM ERNEST. Essays. Macmillan. Rev. Times Lit. Suppl., Feb. 24, 1921. 12s.

407. HENRÍQUEZ UREÑA, P. Sobre J. de L. Ferguson: American Literature in Spain. RFE, 1920, VII, 62–71.

408. HERRICK, ROBERT. New England and the Novel. In The Nation, Sept. 18, 1920, CXI, 323–5.

409. HINE, R. L. The Cream of Curiosity (an account of certain literary and historical MSS of 17, 18 and 19 cent.). London: Routledge. 9 × 6. xvi + 416 pp. 12s. 6d.

410. HOWELLS, WILLIAM DEAN, ed. The Great Modern American Stories: an Anthology; with an introduction. New York: Boni and Livewright. 1920. 8vo. pp. xx + 432. 24 stories that have appeared since 1860.

411. IMELMANN, RUDOLF. Vom romantischen und geschichtlichen Waldef. Engl. St. 53, S. 362–370. Cf. Section IX (b).

412. JAKETOMO, TORAO. American Imitations of Japanese Poetry. In The Nation, Jan. 17, 1920, CX, 70–2.

413. JONES, LLEWELLYN. Free Verse and Its Propaganda In The Sewanee Review, July–Sept. 1920, XXVIII, 384–95.

414. KAYE, FREDERICK B. Puritanism, Literature and War. In The New Republic, Dec. 15, 1920, XXV, 64–7.

415. KER, W. P. The Art of Poetry. (Inaugural lecture at Oxford, June 5.) Oxford: Clarendon Press. 1920. 9¼ × 6. 20 pp. 1s. 6d.

415a. —— The Humanist Ideal. See Essays and Studies by the English Association. X. 392.

416. LANGENFELT, GÖSTA. Sverige och svenskarne i äldre ny-engelsk litteratur. Nordisk Tidskrift för Filologi 1920, 1–2.

417. LATHROP, HENRY BURROWS. The Art of the Novelist. Cr. 8vo. 7¾ × 5. pp. 300. Harrap. 7s. 6d.

418. LAWDER, DONALD. W. L. George on American Literature. In The Bookman, Nov. 1920, LII, 193–7.

419. LAWSON, Mrs ALEXANDER and ALEXANDER (ed. by). A St Andrew's Treasury of Scottish Verse. London: Black. 1920. 7s. 6d.

420. LEWISOHN, LUDWIG. The Poet and His Moment. In The Nation, July 10, 1920, CXI, 42.

421. LOGEMAN, H. Air Songs, in English Studies, vol. II, No. 11, Oct. 1920. pp. 129–31.

422. LOPES, DAVID. Parecer favoravel á publicação nas memorias da Academia do trabalho do sr. Dr. Gustavo Ramos intitulado 'Sobre três tragedias inglesas com motivos portugueses.' V. Boletim da Segunda Classe da Academia das Sciencias, vol. 12°. pags. 370–372. 23·5 × 14·5 cm. Coimbra. 1920.

423. LYND, ROBERT. The Art of Letters. London: Fisher Unwin. 1920. 8¾ × 6. 340 pp. 15s.

423a. —— Old and New Masters. New York: Scribner. 1919. 23 cm. pp. 249, [1]. Dostoevsky the Sensationalist. Jane Austen: Natural Historian. Mr G. K. Chesterton and Mr Hilaire Belloc. Wordsworth. Keats. Henry James. Browning: the Poet of Love. The Fame of J. M. Synge. Villon: the Genius of the Tavern. Pope. James Elroy Flecker. Turgenev. The Madness of Strindberg. 'The Prince of French Poets' [Ronsard]. Rossetti and Ritual. Mr Bernard

Shaw. Mr Masefield's Secret. Mr W. B. Yeats. Tchehov: the Perfect Story-Teller. Lady Gregory. Mr Cunninghame Graham. Swinburne. The Work of T. M. Kettle. Mr J. C. Squire. Mr Joseph Conrad. Mr Rudyard Kipling. Mr Thomas Hardy. Rev. by Philip Goodman in The Bookman, Feb. 1920, L, 614–16.

424. MACPHERSON, W. Principles and Method in the Study of English Literature. Cambridge: Univ. Press. 5s.

425. MADAN, F. Books in Manuscript. (2nd edition.) London: Kegan Paul. 1920. 5s.

426. MAIS, S. P. B. Books and their Writers. London: G. Richards. 7s. 6d.

427. McDOWALL, STEWART. Beauty and the Beast; an Essay in Evolutionary Æsthetic. Cambridge: Univ. Press. 8 × 5½. 93 pp. 7s. 6d.

428. MATTHEWS, BRANDER. The Centenary of a Question. In Scribner's Mag., Jan. 1920, LXVII, 41–6. On Sydney Smith's question, 'Who reads an American Book?'

429. MAURICE, ARTHUR BARTLETT. A New Golden Age in American Reading. In The World's Work, March 1920, XXXIX, 488–507.

429a. —— Literary Landmarks of New York. In The Mentor, Sept. 15, 1920, VIII, 1–11.

430. MENCKEN, HENRY LOUIS. The National Literature. In The Yale Rev., July 1920, IX, 804–17.

431. MOORE, T. STURGE. Some Soldier Poets. New York: Harcourt, Brace and Howe. 1920.

432. MORDELL, A. The Erotic Motive in Literature. New York: Boni and Livewright. 1 dol. 75.

433. MURRY, JOHN MIDDLETON. America and England: a Literary Comparison. In The New Republic, Sept. 8, 1920, XXIV, 41–3.

433a. —— Aspects of Literature. London: Collins. 1920. 9 × 6. ix + 204 pp. 10s.

433b. —— The Condition of English Literature. In The New Republic, May 12, 1920, XXII, 339–41.

434. NEAL, ROBERT WILSON. Short Stories in the Making. [New ed.] New York. Oxford: University Press. [1920.] 19 cm. pp. xiv, 269, [3], 33.

435. NEWBOLT H. A New Study of English Poetry. London: Constable. 9 × 6. vii + 306 pp. 7s. 6d.

436. NITCHIE, ELIZABETH. Vergil and the English Poets. New York: Columbia University Press. 1919. 20·5 cm. pp. x + 251. Columbia Univ. Studies in English and Comp. Lit. Reviewed by Wilfred P. Mustard in Jour. Eng. and Germanic Philol., Apr. 1920, XIX, 298–300; by G. H. C[lark] in The Sewanee Review, Jan.-March 1920, XXVIII, 116–17.

437. O'BRIEN, EDWARD JOSEPH HARRINGTON (ARTHUR MIDDLETON, pseud.). The Best Short Stories of 1919; and the Year Book of the American Short Story. Boston: Small, Maynard & Co. 1920. 8vo. pp. xix + 414.

438. OGLE, MARBURY BLADEN. The Perilous Bridge and Human Automata. Modern Language Notes, XXXV, 3, March 1920, pp. 129–136.

439. O'NEILL, GEORGE. Essays on Poetry. 7½ × 5¼. pp. 138. London: Fisher Unwin; Dublin: Talbot Press. 1920. (Contents: Theory of Poetry; Aubrey de Vere, William Allingham, Thomas Boyd, Gerard Hopkins.) 5s.

440. PARKER, DE WITT H. The Principles of Aesthetics. New York: Silver, Burdett & Co. 1920.

441. PAUL, EDEN and CEDAR. The Appreciation of Poetry. London: Daniel. 7¾ × 5. 59 pp. 2s. 6d.

442. PERRY, BLISS. A Study of Prose Fiction. Revised edition. Boston: Houghton, Mifflin Co. 1920. 19 cm. pp. viii, [4], 406.

442 a. —— A Study of Poetry. Boston: Houghton, Mifflin Co. [1920.] 19 cm. pp. vii, [2], 396. Reviewed by O. W. Firkins in The Weekly Review, Nov. 24, 1920, III, 501–2.

443. PHELPS, W. L. The Advance of English Poetry in the Twentieth Century. London: Allen and Unwin. 1920. Cr. 8vo. 7¾ × 5. pp. 356. 6s. 6d.

444. Poetry Society of America. Books by Twentieth Century Poets. In The Library Journal, Feb. 1, 1920, XLV, 110.

445. POUND, LOUISE. The 'Uniformity' of the Ballad Style. Modern Language Notes, XXXV, 4, April 1920, pp. 217–222.

445 a. —— The English Ballads and the Church. Publications of the Modern Language Association of America, XXXV, 161–188, June 1920.

446. PRICE, LAWRENCE MARSDEN. English and German Literary Influences: Bibliography and Survey. Berkeley, Cal.: University of California Press. 1919–20. 24 × 16 cm. pp. ii + 616. Univ. of California Publications in Modern Philology, IX, 1.

447. QUILLER-COUCH, Sir A. On the Art of Reading. Cambridge: Univ. Press. 1920. viii + 237 pp. 15s.

448. QUINN, ARTHUR HOBSON. Pilgrim and Puritan in Literature. In Scribner's Mag., May 1920, LXVII, 571–81.

449. Romanes Lectures, 1911–1920. Oxford: Clarendon Press. 1920. 16s.

450. ROUTH, H. V. The Origins of the Essay compared in French and English. I, II. Mod. Lang. Review, Jan., April 1920.

451. Royal Society of Literature. Transactions and Report. Vol. XXXVII. 8¾ × 5¾. 202 + 94 pp. Milford. 7s. 1, India in the Literary Renaissance; 2, Modern Indian Poetry (Iusuf Ali); Scotland and France (R. S. Rait); Literature and the State (Sir Edward Brabrook); Some Literary Aspects of France in the War (Edmund Gosse); Effects of Despotism and Freedom on Literature and Medical Ethics (Sir R. H. Charles); Shelley and Calderon (S. de Madariga); Poetry and Time (S. H. Newbolt).

452. RUSSELL, FRANCES THERESA. Satire in the Victorian Novel. Macmillan. xiii + 335 pp. 14s.

453. SAMPSON, G. (ed. by). Cambridge Readings in Literature. Book I, Parts 1 and 2. Cambridge: University Press. 1920. 2s. ea.

454. SCARBOROUGH, DOROTHY. The Supernatural in Modern English Fiction. New York and London: Putnam. vii + 329 pp.

455. SCHRÖER, ARNOLD, M. M. Prof. Dr. Grundzüge und Haupttypen der englischen Literaturgeschichte. 1. Teil von den ältesten Zeiten bis Spenser. 2. Verm. Auflage. Durchges. Neudruck. Sammlung Göschen (1920), No. 286. 160 pp. Berlin: Vereinigung wissensch. Verleger. 4.20 Mk.

456. SCHWEBSCH, ERICH. Schottische Volkslyrik in James Johnson's The Scot's Musical Museum. Palaestra, 95. Unters. u. Texte aus d. deutschen u. engl. Phil. her. v. Alois Brandl, Gustav Roethe und Erich Schmidt. 1920. iv + 218 SS. Gr. 8°. Berlin: Mayer und Müller. 20 Mk.

457. SHERMAN, STUART PRATT. Is There Anything to Be Said for Literary Tradition? In The Bookman, October 1920, LII, 108–12.

458. SMITH, L. PEARSALL (ed. by). A Treasury of English Prose. Constable, London. 1920. 6s.

459. SNYDER, EDWARD DOUGLAS. The Wild Irish: a Study of Some English Satires against the Irish, Scots, and Welsh. In Modern Philology, January 1920, XVII, 687–725.

460. SQUIRE, J. C. Life and Letters. London: Hodder and Stoughton. 1920. 7¾ × 5¼. 298 pp. 7s. 6d.

461. STURGEON, MARY. Studies of Contemporary Poets. New and enlarged edition with Chapters on Thomas Hardy, John Drinkwater, Michael Field, J. C. Squire, W. B. Yeats, and 'Contemporary Women Poets.' Harrap.

462. SWINNERTON, FRANK. The Art of the Novel. In The Bookman, Jan. 1920, L, 411–17.

463. THOMPSON, ELBERT N. S. War Journalism Three Hundred Years Ago. Publications of the Modern Language Association of America, XXXV, 93–115, March 1920.

464. THORNDIKE, ASHLEY HORACE. Literature in a Changing Age. New York: Macmillan. 1920. 20·4 × 14 cm. pp. vi + 318. 18s. Contents: Changing Literature. The Reading Public. The Literary Inheritance. The Literary Environment and Carlyle. Progress and Poverty. Democracy and Empire. Religion. Woman. Science, Invention, and Machinery. Beauty and Art. The Future.

465. TINKER, CHAUNCEY BREWSTER. British Poetry Under the Stress of War. In The Yale Review, July 1920, IX, 714–26.

466. TUPPER, FREDERICK. The Radical in Fiction. In The Review, May 8, 1920, II, 483–5.

467. UNTERMEYER, LOUIS. Sweetness and Light. In The Dial, April 1920, LXVIII, 527–35.

468. VIGLIONE, F. Studi di letteratura italiana, vol. XIII. (Contains an account of Algarotti's criticisms on great English writers.)

469. WARSHAW, JACOB. The Epic-Drama Conception of the Novel.
Modern Language Notes, xxxv, 5, May 1920, pp. 269–279.

470. WEBSTER. Transcendental Points of View: a Survey of the
Criticism of Music, Art, and Letters in The Dial, 1840–1844. In
Washington Univ. Studies, Apr. 1920, VII, 187–203. St Louis.

471. WENDELL, BARRETT. The Traditions of European Literature
from Homer to Dante. New York: Scribner. 1920. 23·5 cm. pp. x+669.

472. WHIBLEY, CHARLES. Literary Portraits. Cr. 8vo. London:
Macmillan & Co.

473. WHITE, NEWMAN I. Racial Traits in the Negro Song. In The
Sewanee Review, July-Sept. 1920, xxviii, 396–404.

474. WHITFORD, ROBERT CALVIN. On the Origin of Probationary
Odes for the Laureateship. Modern Language Notes, xxxv, 2, February 1920, pp. 81–84.

475. WILKINSON, MARGUERITE. New Voices. An Introduction to
Contemporary Poetry. 7¾ × 5¼. pp. xxii+409. Macmillan & Co. 8s. 6d.

476. WILLIAMSON, CLAUDE C. H. Writers of Three Centuries.
London: Grant Richards. 1920. Rev. Times Lit. Suppl., April 1, 1920.
7s. 6d.

477. WILLIAMS, H. Outlines of Modern English Literature.
London: Sidgwick and Jackson. 1920. 7½ × 4¾. 268 pp. 6s.

478. WINBOLT, S. E. The Poetry and Prose of Coleridge, Lamb
and Leigh Hunt. (The Christ's Hospital Anthology.) W. J. Bryce
(Bookseller to Christ's Hospital). xv + 376 pp. 12s. 6d.

479. WINCHESTER, CALEB THOMAS. The New Poetry. In The
Methodist Review, Jan.-Feb. 1920, CIII, 9–21.

480. WORDSWORTH, E. Essays Old and New. Oxford: Clarendon
Press. 7s. 6d.

481. Yale Review, The. American and British Verse from The
Yale Review. With a Foreword by John Gould Fletcher. New
Haven: Yale Univ. Press. 1920. 19·7 × 13·7 cm. pp. 52.

482. ZACHRISSON, EUGEN. Englands främsta diktare (Hardy,
Kipling, Shaw) och världskriget. Ord och Bild XXIX, 5, 1920, pp. 12.
Deals popularly with the works Hardy, Kipling and Shaw have
written bearing on the war and the impression the war has made on
them as seen in their writings (with illustrations) (= the war seen
through different artistic temperaments).

(b) AUTHORS

Barrie, James M. 483. PHELPS, WILLIAM LYON. The Plays of
J. M. Barrie. In The No. Amer. Rev., Dec. 1920, CCXII, 829–43.

Bennett, Arnold. 484. COX, SIDNEY HAYES. Romance in Arnold
Bennett. In The Sewanee Review, July-Sept. 1920, XXVIII, 358–66.

485. Aquests dos. Transl. by Joan d'Albaflor (Josep Carner).
Barcelona: Editorial Catalana. Biblioteca literària, 3 vols. 8vo.
pp. 194, 120, 164.

486. LANOIRE, MAURICE trad. Le ménage Clayhanger. Rev. de Paris. Oct.-Déc. 1920.

487. Sveta i profana ljubav roman jedne mlade žene Zagreb, 1920. Naklada kr. zemaljske tiskare. Zabavna Biblioteka. Uredjuje Dr Nikola Andrić, kolo XIII, knjiga 161–162. 12 × 13. pp. 201. Zena 4 gun.

Brooke, Rupert. 488. DE LA MARE, WALTER. Rupert Brooke and the Intellectual Imagination. New York: Harcourt, Brace and Howe. 1920. 18·5 cm. pp. [ii], 41. Rev. by Christopher Morley in The Book-man, Apr. 1920, LI, 234–5.

489. MANENT, MARIA. A propòsit de Brooke i els poetes de Cam-bridge. Review Monitor Sitges, No. 1, 20 gener 1921.

Burroughs, John. 490. FOERSTER, NORMAN. Burroughs as Berg-sonist. In The No. Amer. Rev., Nov. 1920, CCXII, 670–7.

Chesterton, G. K. 491. CECCHI, EMILIO. Gilbert K. Chesterton. [In] Revista di Milano, Nos. 43, 44, August 5 and 20, 1920. (Milan, 11 Via S. Antonio.)

492. MANENT, MARIA. 'Els savis d'Orient' by G. K. Chesterton (Catalan translation). La Revista, No. de Nadal, 1920, p. 71.

493. TONQUEDEC, J. DE. G. K. Chesterton, ses idées et son caractère. 12 × 19. 128 pp. Nouv. Libr. Nationale. Paris. 5 f.

Conrad, Joseph. 494. KRANENDONK, A. G. VAN. Joseph Conrad, in English Studies, vol. II, No. 7, February 1920, pp. 1–8.

495. NEEL, PHILIPPE trad. Sous les yeux de l'Occident. 14 × 19·5. 310 pp. Nouv. Rev. fr. Paris. 8 f. 25.

496. PUTNAM, GEORGE P. Conrad in Cracow. In The Outlook, March 3, 1920, CXXIV, 382–3.

497. STAWELL, F. MELIAN. Conrad. See Essays and Studies by the English Association, X, 392.

Dobson, Henry Austin. 498. LYMAN, DEAN B., jr. A Little About Austin Dobson. In The Sewanee Review, Jan.-March 1920, XXVIII, 106–8.

Dunsany, Edward John Moreton Drax Plunkett, 18th Baron. 499. HAMILTON, CLAYTON. Lord Dunsany: Personal Impressions. In The Bookman, Feb. 1920, L, 537–42.

Farrington, Harry Webb. 500. ADAMS, FRED WINSLOW. A New Soldier Poet. In The Methodist Review, Jan.-Feb. 1920, CIII, 83–90.

Galsworthy. 501. ALAUX, LOUIS P. trad. Un Saint. 352 pp. 12 × 18. Payot, Paris. 9 f.

502. BIBESCO, LE PRINCE ANTOINE, trad. Le Manoir. Rev. Deux M., Août-Oct. 1920.

503. MATHESIUS, VILÉM. Romány Johna Galsworthyho. I. The Novels of John Galsworthy. Zemĕ, vol. II, 1920–21. 4 n.

Gregory, Lady 504. Visions and Beliefs in the West of Ireland. Collected and arranged by. With two Essays and Notes by W. B. Yeats. 2 vols. Putnam. 22s. 6d.

Haggard, Sir (Henry) Rider. 505. HILLEMACHER, JACQUES trad. Elle. 496 pp. 12 × 18·5. Crès, Paris. 5 f. 50.

506. LABOUCHÈRE, GEORGES trad. (Lettre-préface de M. P. Benoit.) She: Elle. 12 × 19. Edition fr. ill. Paris. 5 f.

507. Хаіару, Сер Рајдер. Она (She). ' Прої реϲ,' 6р. 105–133, 3 септ.—28 окт. 1920. Подлистак.

Hardy, Thomas. 508. ALEXANDER, GRACE. Thomas Hardy, Wizard of Wessex. In The New Republic, Aug. 18, 1920, XXIII, 335–6.

509. BOIVIN, M. H. Les petites ironies de la vie. 304 pp. 11 × 18. Rieder, Paris. 6 f. 75.

510. CHEW, SAMUEL CLAGGETT. Homage to Thomas Hardy. In The New Republic, June 2, 1920, XXIII, 22–6.

511. FAIRLY, B. Notes on the form of The Dynasts. P. M. Lang. Ass. Am. 24, 3.

512. FLETCHER, JOHN GOULD. Thomas Hardy's Poetry: an American View. In Poetry, Apr. 1920, XVI, 43–9.

513. KORTEN, HERTZ. Thomas Hardy's Napoleonsdichtung The Dynasts. Rostocker Diss. 1919, 105 pp. 8°.

Harte, Bret. 514. SAVINE, A. et GEORGES-MICHEL trad. Une épave des plaines. 268 pp. 12 × 19. Edit. fr. ill. Paris. 5 f. 50.

Kipling, Rudyard. 515. BAYO, C. Capitanes valientes. Versión de. 8°. 252 págs. 2.50 ptas.

516. DIXON, JAMES MAIN. Kipling's World Message. In The Methodist Review, July-Aug. 1920, CIII, 525–41.

517. FIRKINS, OLIVER W. Kipling—First and Last Impressions. In The Review, Jan. 31, 1920, II, 109–11.

518. FURNISS, DOROTHY. Quiet Burwash Where Kipling Dwells. In Country Life (Am.), June 1920, XXXVIII, 67–8.

519. MANENT, MARIA. Rudyard Kipling: 'El llibre de la Jungla.' Barcelona: Editorial Catalana. 8vo. pp. 172. (Biblioteca literària.)

520. MAURICE, ARTHUR BARTLETT. About the London of Rudyard Kipling. In The Bookman, Dec. 1920, LII, 311–17.

521. MEAD, GILBERT W. Kipling and Ariosto. Modern Language Notes, XXXV, 2, February 1920, pp. 121–122.

522. SCHULTZ, WILLIAM EBEN. Kipling's Recessional. Modern Language Notes, XXXV, 6, June 1920, p. 375.

523. ROZ, FIRMIN trad. Les yeux de l'Asie. 96 pp. Payot, Paris. 3 f.

McCrae, John. 524. HARMON, H. E. Two Famous Poems of the World War. In The So. Atlantic Quarterly, Jan. 1920, XIX, 9–17. On John McCrae's In Flanders Fields and Alan Seeger's I Have a Rendezvous with Death.

MacGill, Patrick. 525. SNITSLAAR, L. Patrick MacGill, in English Studies, vol. II, No. 8, April 1920.

Masefield, John. 526. FLETCHER, JOHN GOULD. John Masefield: a Study. In The No. Amer. Rev., Oct. 1920, CCXII, 548–51.

527. John Masefield: Que sóc, vida? Mirant. La Rivista, 1920, p. 38.

Merrick, Leonard. 528. An Author's Author. The Nation, Feb. 7, 1920, CX, 177.

Phillips, Stephen. 529. PHILLIPS, HAROLD D. Stephen Phillips in Everyday Life. In The Bookman, Nov. 1920, LII, 213–18.

Pound, Ezra. 530. Ezra Pound: La vinguda de la guerra, Acteu i Ortus. Barcelona: La Revista, 1920, p. 35.

Sassoon, Siegfried. 531. WILKINSON, Mrs MARGUERITE OGDEN BIGELOW (HARLEY GRAVES, pseud.). Siegfried Sassoon. In The Touchstone, May, June 1920, VII, 142–5, 247–8. Port.

Seeger, Alan. 532. HARMON, H. E. Two Famous Poems of the World War. In The So. Atlantic Quarterly, Jan. 1920, XIX, 9–17. On John McCrae's In Flanders Fields and Alan Seeger's I Have a Rendezvous with Death.

Shaw, Bernard. 533. VEDÍA M. DE Y MITRE. El héroe y sus hazañas. Comedia antirromántica. Traducción y notas. Buenos Aires: Cooperativa Editorial. 1920.

534. SKIMPOLE, H. Bernard Shaw: The Man and his work. pp. 192. Allen and Unwin.

535. WEEDA, W. H. Bernard Shaw als Denker, in Stemmen des Tijds, Feb. 1920.

Squire, J. C. 536. OLIVERO, F. Due lirici inglesi d' oggi: W. J. Turner e J. C. Squire. Nuova Antologia, June 16.

Sutro, A. 537. CARNER, JOSEF. 'L' apuntador' by A. Sutro. Catalan translation.

Symons, Arthur. 538. FERRÀ, MIQUEL. Artur Symons: Montserrat, translation into Catalan Verse. In Les Muses Amigues, Sóller, 1920.

Tagore, R. 539. MILLÀS, RAURELL. Rabindranath Tagore: 'The Crescent Moon' in Catalan Verse. In La Veu de Catalunya.

Thompson, Francis. 540. MOREL, A. trad. Étude de M. Wilfrid Meynell. Une antienne de la terre. 45 pp. 21 × 25. Amis du Livre, Paris. 6 f.

541. KRANENDONK, A. G. VAN. Het Dichtwerk van Francis Thompson. Neophilologus, jaargang 5, No. 3, April 1920, p. 231. 22 pp.

542. MAGI, CESARE. Francis Thompson: Il Celeste Segugio—The Hound of Heaven. Versione metrica. 15 pp. 7½ × 5½. Lucca: Tipografia Editrice Baroni. 1920. l. 2.

543. THOMSON, JOHN. Remarks on Francis Thompson's 'Hound of Heaven.' (Paper read Nov. 10, 1919.) 8½ × 5½. 19 pp. Preston: A. Halewood. 6d.

Thomson, James (B.V.). 544. MARKS, JEANNETTE. Disaster and Poetry: a Study of James Thomson (B.V.). In The No. Amer. Rev., July 1920, CCXII, 93–109.

Wells, H. G. 545. The Outline of History; Being a plain History of Life and Mankind. Fol. 11 × 8¼. pp. 384. Cloth, 22s. 6d.; leather, 32s. 6d. G. Newnes. Revised and corrected edition. pp. 672. Cassell. 21s.

546. GUYOT. EDOUARD. H. G. Wells. 304 pp. 14 × 19·5. Payot, Paris. 12 f.

547. **Yeats, W. B.** Visions and Beliefs. See Gregory, Lady, x. 504.

54 BIBLIOGRAPHY

548. DOORN, WILLEM VAN. William Butler Yeats. In English Studies, vol. II, No. 9, June 1920, pp. 65–77.

549. WRENN, C. L. W. B. Yeats: a Literary Study. Reprinted from the Durham University Journal. 9¼ × 7¼. pp. 16. Murby. 1s.

550. ROBINSON, LENNOX. Further Letters of John Butler Yeats. Selected by. 8¼ × 5¾. pp. 81. Co. Dublin: Dundrum & Co, Cuala Press. 12s. 6d.

6. DRAMA

(a) SHAKESPEARE

551. ADAMS, JOSEPH QUINCY. Shakespearean Playhouses. A History of English Theatres from the Beginnings to the Restoration. 8½ × 5¾. xiv + 473 pp. London: Constable. 21s.

552. ACHESON, ARTHUR. Shakespeare's Lost Years in London (1586–1592). London: B. Quaritch. 1920. 9 × 6. vii + 261 pp. 21s.

553. BAKER, G. P. The Development of Shakespeare as a Dramatist. 8vo. x + 329. New York: Macmillan.

554. BAYFIELD, M. A. 'A Study of Shakespeare's Versification' with an inquiry into the trustworthiness of the Early Texts, an examination of the 1616 folio of Ben Jonson's works and appendices, including a revised version of 'Antony and Cleopatra.' Cambridge: University Press. 1920. 9¼ × 6. xii + 521 pp. 16s.

555. BOULENGER, J. L'Affaire Shakespeare. Paris: E. Champion.

556. BRADLEY, HENRY. Note on Cursed Hebenon (or Hebona). Mod. Lang. Rev., 1920, vol. XV, pp. 85–87.

557. BROOKE, STOPFORD A. On Ten Plays of Shakespeare. London: Constable. 1920. 8¼ × 5½. 311 pp. 7s. 6d.

557a. —— Ten More Plays of Shakespeare. London: Constable. 1920. 8¼ × 5½. 313 pp. 7s. 6d.

558. CASTELAIN, MAURICE. Shakespeare ou Derby? Revue Germanique, pp. 1-39, No. 1, 1920.

559. Catalan Translations: (1) Hamlet in Catalan Verse, by Magi Morera i Galicia. Barcelona: Biblioteca Literària. Rev. Jordi March 'La Veu de Catalunya,' 24 March 1920, in La Revista, 1920, p. 96. (2) Rumea i Julieta, by id. (3) Sonnet by id. in Messidor, 1918–1920, p. 353.

560. CHAPMAN, WILLIAM HALL. Shakespeare: the Personal Phase. Los Angeles, Calif. Privately printed. 1920. 8vo. pp. xix + 403. Front., plates. 500 copies printed.

561. COLLISON-MORLEY, LACY. Shakespeare in Italy. pp. 180. Stratford.

562. COULTER, CORNELIA CATLIN. The Plautine Tradition in Shakespeare. In Journal of Eng. and Germanic Philol., Jan. 1920, XIX, 66–83.

563. CRAWFORD, J. P. WICKERSHAM. A Sixteenth-Century Spanish Analogue of Measure for Measure. Modern Language Notes, XXXV, 6, June 1920, pp. 330–334.

564. CRAWFORD, J. R. (ed. by). As You Like It (The Yale Shakespeare). New Haven: Yale Univ. Press. London: Milford. 6¼ × 4½. 146 pp. 4s. 6d.

565. CROCE, B. Ariosto, Shakespeare e Corneille. Bari, Laterza. L. 16.50.

566. DOBELL, P. J. Some Seventeenth-Century Allusions to Shakespeare and his works not hitherto collected. London: Dobell. 1920. 3s.

567. ENK, P. J. Shakespeare's 'Small Latin.' Neophilologus, jaargang 5, p. 359, 5 pp.

568. FEHR, B. Shakespeare und Coventry. Anglia, Beibl. 31, S. 85–7.

569. FIRKINS, OSCAR W. What Happened to Hamlet? A New Phase of an Old View. In The No. Amer. Rev., Sept. 1920, CCXII, 393–403.

570. FORSYTHE, ROBERT STANLEY. A Plautine Source of The Merry Wives of Windsor. In Modern Philology, Dec. 1920, XVIII, 401–21.

571. FURNESS, HORACE HOWARD (jun.) (ed. by). The Life and Death of King John (A new variorum edition). London: Lippincott. 1920. 9¾ × 6¾. xiii + 728 pp. 25s.

571a. —— A New Variorum Edition of Shakespeare. The Life and Death of King John. Philadelphia: J. B. Lippincott Co. 1919 [1920]. 25 × 18 cm. pp. xiii, [1], 728. Reviewed by Samuel C. Chew in Amer. Jour. Philol., Jan.-March 1920, XLI, 81–4.

572. GIDE, ANDRÉ trad. Antoine et Cléopâtre. Nouv. Rev. Française. Juillet-Septembre 1920.

573. GUNDOLF, FRIEDRICH. Shakespeare und der deutsche Geist. 5. unveränd. Auflage, 9.–13. Taus. 1920. VIII, 359 pp. Gr. 8°. Berlin: G. Bondi. 30 Mk.

574. GRADWOHL, REBECCA J. The Children of Shakespeare's Dramas. In The Catholic World, April 1920, CXI, 77–85.

575. GRAY, HENRY DAVID. The Titus Andronicus Problem. In Studies in Philology, April 1920, XVII, 126–31.

575a. —— Did Shakespeare write a Tragedy of 'Dido'? Modern Lang. Review, July 1920.

575b. —— The Sources of The Tempest. Modern Language Notes, XXXV, 6, June 1920, pp. 321–330.

576. GREENWOOD, Sir GEORGE. Shakespeare's Handwriting. London: J. Lane. 1920. 8½ × 5½. 36 pp. 2s.

576a. —— Shakespeare's Law. London: Cecil Palmer. 1920. 7½ × 5. 48 pp. 2s. 6d.

577. HERFORD, C. H. The Normality of Shakespeare, illustrated in his treatment of Love and Marriage. The English Association. 1920. 9¾ × 6. 1s.

577a. —— Othello: The Moor of Venice. The Warwick Shakespeare. 18mo. 6¼ × 4½. pp. 214. Blackie. 2s. 6d.

578. HUBBARD, FRANK G. The First Quarto Edition of Shakespeare's Hamlet. Edited with an Introduction and Notes. Madison, Wis. 1920. 25 × 16·3 cm. pp. 120. University of Wisconsin Studies in Language and Literature 8.

579. Jahrbuch der Deutschen Shakespeare-Gesellschaft her. v. Wolfgang Keller. 56. Jahrgang. Berlin u. Leipzig: Vereinigung Wissenschaftlicher Verleger. iv + 156. Gr. 8°. JÜRGENS, WOLDEMAR. Die Inszenierung von Shakespeare's Lustspielen. 8–24. LUDWIG, A. Nietzsche und Shakespeare. 24–58. KILIAN, EUGEN. 'Mass für Mass' als deutscher Bühnenstück. 58–73. LEITZMANN, A. Karl Lachmann als Shakespeare-Übersetzer. 73–90. KELLER, W. Die Anordnung von Shakespeare's Dramen in der ersten Folio-Ausgabe. 90–95. HIRSCHBERG, JULIUS. Shakespeare-Anmerkungen einer Augenarztes. 95–106. KELLER, WOLFGANG. Der Schluss von Sh.'s Troilus und Cressida. 106. HIRSCHBERG, JUL. The Valley (Winter's Tale, II, 3, 100). 107. Nekrologe, Bücherschen, Theaterschau. 115–153.

580. JORGA, N. Istoria Literaturilor Romanice, vol. II. 293–422 pp. 22 × 16. Editura Pavel Suru, Bucureşti. 1920. 35 lei. As shown by the title, Professor Jorga, dealing with the history of Romanic Literature all over Europe, tries to find out the various influences of Italian, French and Spanish literatures on Spenser's Fairy Queen and Shakespeare's works.

581. KELLY, F. J. Shakespeare and the Art of Music. In The Catholic World, Jan. 1920, CX, 498–503.

582. KENYON, JOHN SAMUEL. Hamlet, III, iv, 64. Modern Language Notes, XXXV, 1, January 1920, pp. 50–52.

583. KINGSLEY, MAUDE ELMA. Outline Study of Shakespeare's King John. In Education, Nov. 1920, XLI, 176–91.

584. LANDAUER, GUSTAV. Shakespeare. Dargestellt in Vorträgen. 2 Bde (VII, 352 u. 395 pp.). 8°. Frankfurt (Main). 82 Mk.

585. LANDAU, L. Some Parallels to Shakespeare's Seven Ages. In Jour. Eng. and Germ. Philcl., July 1920, XIX, 382–96.

586. LANGENFELT, G. Danzig och Dansk. Finsk Tidskrift. 1920. pp. 63–79.

587. LAWRENCE, W. J. The Masque in 'The Tempest.' Fortn. Rev., June.

587a. —— The Mystery of Macbeth. Fortn. Rev., Nov. 1920.

588. LAWRENCE, WILLIAM WITHERLE. The Wager in Cymbeline. In Publ. Mod. Lang. Assn America, Dec. 1920, XXXV, 391–431.

589. LEFRANC, ABEL. La réalité dans le Songe d'une Nuit d'Été (Mélanges B. Bouvier). Sonor, Genève, 1920. Tirage à part (100 ex.) avec note additionnelle.

589a. —— Le secret du Songe d'une Nuit d'Été. Opinion, 16 et 23 Oct. 1920. Illustration, 30 Oct. 1920.

590. LEVEY, S. The Tempest, what led up to it and what followed. Information derived from many sources. London: Fountain Publ. Co. 1s.

591. LOONEY, J. THOMAS. Shakespeare Identified. New York: Frederick A. Stokes Co. [1920.] 24 cm. pp. x, [2], 466. Front., ports. Identifies S. as Edward de Vere, Earl of Oxford. Rev. by Joseph Krutch in The Nation, Aug. 28, 1920, CXI, 248–9.

592. —— 'Shakespeare' Identified in Edward de Vere, 17th Earl of Oxford. London: Palmer and Hayward. 1920. 9 × 5¼. 551 pp. 21s.

593. MCNAIR, ARNOLD. Shakespeare and Dr Caius. From The Caian (the magazine of Caius College, Cambridge), vol. XXVIII, 1920.

594. MASELLI, A. Gli Umili nella tragedia greca e Shakespeariana. Alatti, Isola.

595. MOWAT, R. B. Henry V. London: Constable. 1920. 10s. 6d.

596. ODELL, GEORGE C. D. Shakespeare from Betterton to Irving. New York: Scribner. 1920. Large 8vo. 2 vols. Illus. Rev. by Montrose J. Moses in The Nation, Dec. 8, 1920, CXI, 660, 664.

597. OESTERBERG, V. Studier over Hamlet. Teksterne I. Gyldendal, Copenhaguen and London. 8vo. pp. 74.

598. POLLARD, A. W. Shakespeare's Fight with the Pirates and the Problems of the Transmission of his Text. (2nd edit. Revised with Introduction.) Cambridge: University Press. 7½ × 5¼. xxviii + 110 pp. 7s. 6d.

598a. —— The Variant Settings in 2 Henry IV and their Spelling. Times Lit. Suppl., Oct. 21, 1920.

599. POLLEN, FOX. Shakespeare and Benelli. In Arts and Decoration, Apr. 1920, XII, 396–7.

600. REA, JOHN D. Notes on Shakespeare. Modern Language Notes, XXXV, 6, June 1920, pp. 377–378.

600a. —— A Note on The Tempest. Modern Language Notes, XXXV, 5, May 1920, pp. 313–315.

601. REYHER, PAUL. Alfred de Vigny, Shakespeare et G. de Montemayor. [As You Like It, IV, i, 147.] Rev. de l'Ens. des Langues Vivantes, No. 1, Janv. 1920.

602. ROLLAND, ROMAIN. Die Wahrheit in dem Werke Shakespeares. (Aus dem Franz. übers. v. Hannah Szász.) 51 pp. 8°. Berlin, 1920.

602a. —— Shakespeare the Truthteller. Translated by Helena Van Brugh de Kay. In The Dial, August 1920, LXIX, 109–21.

603. RUSSELL, CHARLES EDWARD. Hamstringing Shakespeare. In The Bookman, Nov. 1920, LII, 207–12.

604. SCHAUBERT, ELSE VON. Drayton's Anteil an Heinrich VI, 2. und 3. Teil. Neue Anglistische Arbeiten her. v. Levin L. Schücking und Max Deutschlein, No. 4. 1920. xvi + 219. Gr. 8°. Köthen: O. Schulze. 30 Mk.

605. SCHÜCKING, LEVIN L. Die Charakterprobleme bei Shakespeare. Leipzig: Tauchnitz. 7 M. Rev. Times Lit. Suppl., Feb. 5, 1920.

606. SCHULZE, KONRAD. Zu Chaucers 'Weib von Bath' und Shakespeares 'Kaufmann von Venedig.' G.R.M. VIII, 103–105.

58 BIBLIOGRAPHY

Translations. 607. Obras completas. Traducción de R. Martínez
Lafuente. Valencia: Edit. Prometeo. 8°. 12 vols.

608. Hamlet. Traducción de M. Morera Galicia. Barcelona. 8°.
183 págs. 2 ptas.

609. Hamlet: Romeo y Julieta. Traducción sor Roviralta Borrel.
Barcelona: Editorial Ibérica.

610. Romeo y Julieta. Traducción de G. Martínez Sierra. 12°.
198 págs. 4 ptas.

611. La tragedia de Hamlet, príncipe de Dinamarca. Traducción
de G. Martínez Sierra. 12°. 213 págs. 4 ptas.

612. La tragedia de Macbeth. La traducción del inglés ha sido
Mecha por L. Astrana Marín. Madrid: Tip. Renovación. 1920. 8°.
175 págs. 1 pta. Colección Universal (Calpe).

613. BOGDANOVIC, MILAN. Julije Cezar. Tragedija u 5 činova
(Mat. hrv.). Zagreb, 1920. 8°. 148 str., broš.

614. Sen kresne noči. Ljubljana 1920. Preveo sengleskog Otto
Župančić. Tiskarna Zadruge. 128 strana. Cena 22 krune.

615. MACBETH. Tragedija u 5 činova. Sengleskog preveo Vl.
Nazor. Suvodom o životu i djelima W. Shakespeare—a od Vl. Dukata.
Broširano K. 2.

616. Otelo. Preveo Dr. Milan Bogdanović. Izdanje Matice
Hrvatske. Cena K. 6.

617. Kralij Lear. Preveo Dr. Milan Bogdanović. Zagreb, 1919.
Izvanredno izdanje M. N. 8-ina. 195 str. Cijena K. 8.

618. Julije Cezar. Tragedija u 5 činova. Preveo Dr. Milan Bogdanović, izdanje Matice Hrvatske. Zagreb, 1920. 8-ina. 148
strana.

619. SERRURIER, C. Voltaire et Shakespeare. A propos du Mono-
logue d'Hamlet. Neophilologus, jaargang 5, April 1920, p. 205, 5 pp.

620. SGROI, C. Nuova luce su W. Shakespeare. Rassegna italiana,
July 31–Aug. 31.

621. SHARP, R. F. Travesties of Shakespeare's Plays. Library, 4th
ser., I, I, June 1920.

622. SHORE, W. TEIGNMOUTH. Shakespeare's Self. London:
Philip Allan & Co. 1920. 7¾ × 5. 186 pp. 5s.

623. STEVENSON, W. H. Shakespeare's Schoolmaster and Handwriting. Times Lit. Suppl., Jan. 8, 1920.

624. STOLL, ELMER EDGAR. Hamlet: an Historical and Comparative Study. Minneapolis: Univ. of Minnesota. 1920. 10 × 6¾. 76 pp.
$1.00.

625. SYKES, H. DUGDALE. The Authorship of 'The Taming of the
Shrew,' 'The Famous Victories of Henry V' and the additions to
Marlowe's 'Faustus.' (For the Shakespearean Association.) London:
Chatto and Windus. 1920. 9¾ × 6¼. 35 pp. 1s. 6d.

626. SYMONS, ARTHUR. On Hamlet and Hamlets. In The Nation,
July 24, 1920, CXI, 97–8.

627. THOMPSON, JAMES WESTFALL. Shakespere and Puritanism. In The No. Am. Rev., Aug. 1920, CCXII, 228–37.

628. TIECK, LUDWIG. Das Buch über Shakespeare. Handschriftliche Aufzeichnungen. Aus dem Nachlass her. v. Henry Lüdeke. No. 1 der Neudrucke deutscher Literaturwerke des 18. und 19. Jahrh. her. v. A. Leitzmann und Waldemar Oehlke. xxvi + 524 pp. Halle: Niemeyer. 36 Mk.

629. VULLIAND, PAUL. Le mythe shakespearien. Mercure de Fr., vol. CXXXIX, pp. 5–33, 1920.

630. WILLIAMS, STANLEY T. Some Versions of Timon of Athens on the Stage. In Modern Philology, September 1920, XVIII, 269–85.

630 a. —— (ed. by). Life of Timon of Athens. New Haven: Yale Univ. Press. London: Milford. 1920. 18mo. 6¾ × 4½. 141 pp. 4s. 6d.

631. WOLFF, MAX J. Italienisches bei Shakespeare. Engl. Stud. 54, 473.

631 a. —— Der dramatische Begriff der 'History' bei Shakespeare. Engl. Stud. 54, 194–201.

632. WOLFFHARDT, ELISABETH. Shakespeare und das Griechentum. Berliner Dissert. von 1920. vii + 55 pp. Berlin: Mayer u. Müller.

633. WOODBRIDGE, STOWER E. The Yale Shakespeare. In Jour. Eng. and Germ. Philol., July 1920, XIX, 426–30.

(b) SIXTEENTH—TWENTIETH CENTURY DRAMA (EXCL. SHAKESPEARE)

I. ENGLISH

634. ARCHER, W. The Duchess of Malfi. The Nineteenth Century, Jan. 1920.

635. BASKERVILL, CHARLES READ. Dramatic Aspects of Medieval Folk Festivals in England. In Studies in Philology, January 1920, XVII, 19–87.

636. BATEMAN, MAY. Drama with an Ideal. In The Catholic World, June 1920, CXI, 318–29.

637. BOAS, F. S. 'Hamlet and Volpone' at Oxford. Fortn. Rev., May 1920.

637 a. —— Stage Censorship under Charles II: Sir Henry Herbert and The Cheats. Times Lit. Suppl., April 15, 22, 1920. Cf. Summers, Montague. ib. April 29.

638. BRERETON, J. LE ROY. One-Door Interiors on the Elizabethan Stage. Modern Language Notes, XXXV, 2, February 1920, pp. 119–120.

639. BROOKE, CHARLES FREDERICK TUCKER. Elizabethan 'Nocturnal' and 'Infernal' Plays. Modern Language Notes, XXXV, 2, February 1920, pp. 120–121.

640. BROWN, CARLETON FAIRCHILD, ed. The Stonyhurst Pageants. Baltimore: The Johns Hopkins Press, 1920. 24 × 16·5 cm. pp. 30, 302. Hesperia: Supplementary Series 7.

641. BRUCE, HAROLD L. Is Comedy Free? In The Sewanee Review, July-Sept. 1920, XXVIII, 438–43.·

642. CANNAN, GILBERT. The English Theatre During and After the War. In The Theatre Arts Mag., Jan. 1920, IV, 21–4.

643. CLARK, BARRETT HARPER. A Study Outline of Plays with a Purpose, Dealing with an Ethical Truth. In The Drama, Jan. 1920, X, 167.

644. CORDEIRO RAMOS, GUSTAVO. Sobre três tragedias inglesas com motivos portugueses. V. Historia e Memorias da Academia das Sciencias de Lisboa, nova serie, 2ª classe, tomo XIV, No. 6. Coimbra. 1920. 199 pags. 30·5 × 23 cm.

645. CRAWFORD, JACK RANDALL. Pageant Technique. In Quart. Jour. Speech Education, Feb. 1920, VI, 1, 76–8.

646. CREW, HELEN COALE. Behold a Great Hiatus. In The Drama, Dec. 1920, XI, 77–9.

647. CROCKER, LOUIS. A Note on Comedy. In The Nation, Sept. 25, 1920, CXI, 347–8.

648. CRUICKSHANK, A. H. Philip Massinger. Oxford: Blackwell. 1920. 8¾ × 5¾. vii + 228 pp. 15s.

648a. —— Philip Massinger. New York: Frederick A. Stokes Co. 1920.

649. DICKINSON, THOMAS H. The Contemporary Drama of England. 8vo. 8 × 5¼. pp. 303. J. Murray. 1920. 7s. 6d.

650. FERGUSON, A. S. The Plays of George Chapman. II. Mod. Lang. Review, July 1920.

651. COSTA, FERNANDES. Infiltração da litteratura hespanhola, mormente a dramatica, nas letras inglesas, desde o corneço do seculo XV até hoje. V. Boletim da Segunda Classe da Academia das Sciencias, vol. 12°. pags. 565–586. 23·5 × 14·5 cm. Coimbra. 1920.

652. FISCHER, WALTHER. Zur Biographie Kaspar Heywoods. Engl. Stud. 54, 352–358.

653. Gammer Gurtons Nedle, by Mr. S. Mr. of Art. Ed. by H. F. B. Brett-Smith. Boston: Houghton, Mifflin Co. 1920. 12mo. pp. xv + 79. The Percy Reprints, No. 2.

654. GILBERT, ALLAN H. Milton and the Mysteries. In Studies in Philology, Apr. 1920, XVII, 147–69.

655. GOVINDA RAO, C. K. Scott's Ivanhoe Dramatised. pp. 87. 8°. Published by the author at Ramachandrapuram, 1920. Price 8 annas.

656. GRAVES, THORNTON SHIRLEY. The Elizabethan Trained Ape. Modern Language Notes, XXXV, 4, April 1920, pp. 248–249.

656a. —— Notes on the Elizabethan Theatres. In Studies in Philology, April 1920, XVII, 170–82.

656b. —— Richard Rawlidge on London Playhouses. In Modern Philology, May 1920, XVIII, 41–7.

656c. —— The Devil in the Playhouse. In The So. Atlantic Quarterly, April 1920, XIX, 131–40.

656*d*. GRAVES, THORNTON SHIRLEY. Organized Applause. In The So. Atlantic Quarterly, July 1920, XIX, 236–48.

657. GROSSMANN, RUD. Spanien und das elisabethanische Drama. (Hamburgische Universität, Abhandl. aus dem Gebiet der Auslandskunde, Bd. 4.) Hamburg. 1920. 138 pp.

658. HAMILTON, CLAYTON. Problems of the Playwright. 7½ × 5¼. pp. xiii + 339. London: Allen and Unwin. 7s. 6d.

659. HENDERSON, ARCHIBALD. The Drama—After the War. In The So. Atlantic Quarterly, July 1920, XIX, 258–65.

660. HILLEBRAND, HAROLD N. The Early History of the Chapel Royal. In Modern Philology, September 1920, XVIII, 233–68.

661. HUGHES, GLENN. Concerning a Theatre of the People. In The Drama, Nov. 1920, XI, 45–6.

662. KOBERG, WERNER. Quellenstudien zu John Crowne's 'Darius.' Kieler Diss. 142 pp. 8°.

663. LAWRENCE, W. J. Elizabethan 'Motions.' Times Lit. Suppl., Jan. 29, 1920. Cf. C. Stuart Allison. Ib. Feb. 12; W. J. Lawrence, Feb. 19; Alwin Thaler, Feb. 26.

663*a*. —— Music in the Elizabethan Theatre. In The Musical Quarterly, Apr. 1920, VI, 192–205.

663*b*. —— The Authorship of 'Fedele and Fortunio.' Times Literary Supplement, May 20, 1920.

664. LEWISOHN, LUDWIG. Toward a People's Theatre. In The Nation, Jan. 17, 1920, CX, 80–2.

664*a*. —— The Cult of Violence. In The Nation, Jan. 24, 1920, CX, 118.

664*b*. —— Play-Making. In The Nation, Feb. 28, 1920, CX, 270.

664*c*. —— Underworld. In The Nation, Oct. 6, 1920, CXI, 383.

664*d*. —— Balance Sheet. In The Nation, June 12, 1920, CX, 806–7.

665. LIEBERMANN, F. Zwischenspiele für Edward II. Archiv 140, 262.

666. LOCKERT, LACY. A Scene in The Fatal Dowry. (Philip Massinger and Nathaniel Field. The Fatal Dowry.) Modern Language Notes, XXXV, 5, May 1920, pp. 291–293.

667. LYLE, MARIE CAROLINE. The Original Identity of the York and Towneley Cycles. Minneapolis: Univ. of Minnesota. 1919. 25·5 cm. pp. iv, [2], 113. Research Publs. Univ. of Minnesota, VIII, 3. Rev. by Grace Frank in Mod. Lang. Notes, Jan. 1920, XXXV, 45–8.

668. MATTHEWS, BRANDER. Playwrights on Playwriting. In The No. Amer. Rev., Oct. 1920, CCXII, 552–60.

668*a*. —— Tragedies with Happy Endings. In The No. Amer. Rev., March 1920, CCXI, 355–65.

668*b*. —— Telescoping Time in the Theatre. In The Bookman, Jan. 1920, L, 467–73.

669. MCCALLUM, J. D. Greene's Friar Bacon and Friar Bungay. Modern Language Notes, XXXV, 4, April 1920.

670. MILLER, FRANCES H. Stanzaic Division in York Play XXXIX. Modern Language Notes, XXXV, 6, June 1920, pp. 379–380.

671. MORIN, PILAR. Silent dramą and its application to the spoken word. In Amer. Phys. Educa. Rev., Jan. 1920, XXV, 13–14.

672. NASON, A. H. James Shirley, Dramatist: a biographical and critical study. New York: University Press.

673. NICOLL, ALLARDYCE. Doors and Curtains in Restoration Theatres. Mod. Lang. Review, April 1920.

673a. —— The Origin and Types of the Heroic Tragedy. Anglia, 44, 325–337.

673b. —— Scenery in Restoration Theatres. Anglia, 44, 217–226.

674. NICHOLS, CHARLES W. A Note on The Stage-Mutineers. Modern Language Notes, XXXV, 4, April 1920, pp. 225–227.

675. OLSON, BEATRICE. The Morris Dance in Drama before 1640. In Quart. Journal of the Univ. of No. Dakota, July 1920, X, 422–35.

676. PATCH, HOWARD R. The Ludus Coventriae and the Digby Massacre. Publications of the Modern Language Association of America, XXXV, 324–343, September 1920.

677. PHELPS, WILLIAM LYON. The Plays of J. M. Barrie. In The No. Amer. Rev., Dec. 1920, CCXII, 829–43.

678. RICHTER, HELENE. G. B. Shaws Dramen aus der Kriegszeit. Germ.-Rom.-Monatsschrift, VIII, 290–299. Heidelberg. 1920.

679. RÖHRICHT, IRMGARD, Dr. Frauenprobleme in der englischen Literatur. 1. Das Idealbild der Frau bei Philipp Massinger, 1920, III, 121. 8°. München: Piloty u. Loehle. 5 Mk.

680. ROLLINS, HYDER EDWARD. William Elderton: Elizabethan Actor and Ballad-Writer. In Studies in Philology, April 1920, XVII, 199–245.

681. ROSS, CLARENDON. A Note on the Lack of Theatricality in Modern Realistic Drama. In The Drama, Jan. 1920, X, 156–8.

682. SCHARPFF, PAULUS. Über ein englisches Auferstehungspiel. Ein Beitrag zur Geschichte des Dramas und der Lollarden. Winnenden. 1920. 63 pp. 8°. Erlanger Diss.

683. SCHOELL, F. L. Charlemagne: The Distracted Emperor. Drame Elisabethain Anonyme. Roy. 8vo. Oxford: University Press. 12s. 6d.

684. SCHWEMMER, PAUL. John Bales Drama: A brefe Comedy or Enterlude concernynge the temptacyon of our lorde and sauer Jesus Christ by Sathan in the desart. Nürnberg. 1919. Erlanger Diss. 1920.

685. SHAY, FRANK, and PIERRE LOVING, eds. Fifty Contemporary One-Act Plays. Cincinnati: Stewart and Kidd Co. 1920. 21·5 × 15·3 cm. pp. viii + 582.

686. SMITH, HESTER TRAVERS. Drama in Ireland, 1919–1920. In The Drama, June 1920, X, 308–9.

687. SYMONS, ARTHUR. Stevenson Again on the Stage. The Literary Digest. Oct. 9, 1920, LXVII, 2, 32–3. On a dramatization of The Master of Ballantrae.

688. SWAEN, A. E. H. Thersytes. Neophilologus, jaargang 5, p. 160. 2½ pp.

689. SYMONS, ARTHUR. Studies in the Elizabethan Drama. London: Heinemann. 1920. 8¼ × 5¼. 261 pp. Rev. Times Lit. Suppl., May 6. 12s.

690. TAFT, LINWOOD. The Technique of Pageantry. In The Drama, July-Sept. 1920, X, 365–72.

691. THALER, ALWIN. The Elizabethan Dramatic Companies. Publications of the Modern Language Association of America, XXXV, 123–159, March 1920.

692. —— Milton in the Theatre. In Studies in Philology, July 1920, XVII, 269–308.

692 a. —— The 'Free-List' and Theatre Tickets in Shakespeare's Time and After. Mod. Lang. Review, April 1920.

692 b. —— The Players at Court, 1564–1642. In Journal of Eng. and Germanic Philol., January 1920, XIX, 19–46.

692 c. —— The Travelling Players in Shakspere's England. In Modern Philology, Jan. 1920, XVII, 489–514.

693. TISDEL, FREDERICK MONROE. Symbolism in the Theatre. In The Sewanee Review, April-June 1920, XXVIII, 228–40.

694. TUFFER, F. and W. (ed. by). Representative English Dramas from Dryden to Sheridan; selected and edited. Oxford: University Press. 1920. 466 pp. 6s. 6d.

695. VAN DOREN, MARK. England's Rarest. In The Nation, Feb. 14, 1920, CX, 206. A review of G. Gregory Smith's Ben Jonson and Percy Simpson's ed. of Every Man in His Humour.

696. WALKLEY, A. B. The English Actor of To-Day. In The Yale Rev., Apr. 1920, IX, 542–54.

697. WEBSTER, JOHN. La duquesa de Malfi. Tragedia. Traducción de E. Díez-Canedo. Madrid: Tipográfica Renovación. 1920. 8°. 192 págs. 1 pta. Colección Universal (Calpe).

698. WITHINGTON, ROBERT. Scott's Contribution to Pageantic Development—a Note on the Visit of George IV to Edinburgh in 1822. In Studies in Philology, April 1920, XVII, 121–5.

699. WHITNEY, ANNE T. Drama in the Industries. In The Drama, Nov. 1920, XI, 62–4.

700. WHITWORTH, GEOFFREY. The British Drama League. In The Drama, Oct. 1920, XI, 9–10.

2. AMERICAN

701. Poetry Society of America. List of 20th Century American Poetic Drama. In The Library Journal, May 1, 1920, XLV, 395–6.

702. ALLEN, BEVERLY SPRAGUE. William Godwin and the Stage. In Publ. Mod. Lang. Assn America, Sept. 1920, XXXV, 358–74.

703. ANDREWS, HAZEL M. Vocational and Moral Guidance Through Dramatics. In Education, Oct. 1920, XLI, 123–31.

704. ARCHER, WILLIAM. The Development of the American Drama. In Harper's, Dec. 1920, CXLII, 75–86.

705. BAKER, GEORGE PIERCE, ed. Modern American Plays, with an Introduction. New York: Harcourt, Brace and Howe. 1920. pp. x + 544. Includes As a Man Thinks, The Return of Peter Grimm, Romance.

706. BURTON, RICHARD EUGENE. Theatre Activities in Southern California. In The Theatre Arts Mag., Oct. 1920, IV, 346–7.

707. COAD, ORAL SUMNER. Stage and Players in Eighteenth Century America. In Journal of Eng. and Germanic Philol., Apr. 1920, XIX, 201–23.

708. CRAIG, EDWARD GORDON. The Theatre-Advancing. Boston: Little, Brown & Co. 21 cm. pp. vii + 298. Illus. Rev. by Oliver M. Sayler in The New Republic, July 14, 1920, XXIII, 206–7.

709. DRUMMOND, ALEXANDER M. A countryside theatre experiment. In Quart. Jour. Speech Education, Feb. 1920, VI, 1, 44–7.

710. EATON, WALTER PRICHARD. Playwrights and Professors. In The Theatre Arts Mag., Jan. 1920, IV, 16–20.

711. HAMILTON, CLAYTON. Seen on the Stage. New York: Henry Holt & Co. 1920.

712. LEWIS, BENJAMIN ROLAND. The One-Act Play in Colleges and High Schools, with Bibliographies and a List of One-Act Plays for Study and Production. Salt Lake City: University of Utah. [1920.] 23 cm. pp. 25. Bulletin of the University of Utah, x, 16.

713. MACGOWAN, KENNETH. American Drama Mid-Channel. In The Theatre Arts Mag., Jan. 1920, IV, 3–15.

Printed in the United States
By Bookmasters